Make the system work for YOU!

One out of three people in the United States, after having maintained good credit for years, will get into some kind of credit bind that will reflect on them for years, even a lifetime. And it's not just a matter of reputation. An unresolved credit problem could cost you your home . . .

Fortunately, there are things you can do . . . It's a relatively simple matter of determining what your credit files say about you and then following through to set the record straight, assert your legal rights, or negotiate settlement of an outstanding debt *on terms you can manage* in exchange for a restored good credit rating.

You can do it. You don't have to be a victim of the system. You *can* make the system work for you.

Here's how.

PEARL POLTO'S
EASY GUIDE TO
GOOD CREDIT

PEARL POLTO'S
EASY GUIDE TO GOOD CREDIT

PEARL B. POLTO
WITH BOB OSKAM

BERKLEY BOOKS, NEW YORK

PEARL POLTO'S EASY GUIDE TO GOOD CREDIT

A Berkley Book / published by arrangement with
the author

PRINTING HISTORY
Berkley trade paperback edition / March 1990
Berkley mass market edition / May 1996

The Putnam Berkley World Wide Web site address is
http://www.berkley.com

ISBN: 0-425-15297-9

Contents

Introduction

If you are caught committing a crime, you pay a price—a term in a jail cell. When your term is up, you are released; there is no longer an outstanding charge against you, and you are free to pursue your hopes and dreams like any other citizen.

But if ever you are ruled to be a poor credit risk, you may well find yourself saddled with a lifetime sentence. No matter what the reason for your failure to maintain a creditworthy status—you may have suffered a debilitating illness or lost your job—you'll find yourself regarded and treated as a deadbeat. Any application for credit, from a department store charge card to a car loan or home mortgage, will be met with a curt refusal. And no one will care that you have an explanation or are prepared to demonstrate good faith. As far as any creditor is concerned, you're just another bum who can't be trusted.

Millions of people of good character and basic integrity find themselves in this situation. One out of three people in the United States, after having maintained good credit for years, will get into some kind of credit bind that will reflect on them for years, even a life-time. And it's not just a matter of reputation. An un-resolved credit problem could cost you your home.

As if all that weren't bad enough, today's consumer credit system routinely overlooks or ignores legal safe-guards designed to protect consumers who experience credit difficulties. More often than not, no one calls the creditor or credit agency to account, the abuses con-tinue, and people's lives are irreparably damaged.

Sometimes the difficulty you experience with re-spect to credit has nothing to do with any failure on your part. A credit agency may simply decide you don't have what it takes and arbitrarily condemn you to a second-class kind of economic existence. You can't get credit because you have no credit. In other cases, there's an error in the system itself that affects your rating. It won't be your fault, but you're the one who pays the price, who can't arrange a new car loan or get a mortgage to buy that long-dreamed-of family home.

The average individual faced with credit problems feels powerless when confronted with a system that so obviously doesn't care. And because creditors and credit agencies so clearly have economic might on their side—and continually invoke their economic right—the average individual assumes there's really little that can be done to salvage or improve a sorry situation.

Fortunately there are things you can do. You do have rights as a consumer. While the system appears in most ways to be weighted against you, there are laws protecting you from being permanently branded as a bad credit risk. You don't have to serve a lifelong sentence in an economic prison whose keys are in the hand of an all-powerful credit system. And although you may count it for little, you do have some power of your own—the power of the consumer, whose economic decisions ultimately support the whole structure upon which the credit system rests.

Surprisingly, clearing yourself of a bad credit rating isn't as complicated a procedure as it seems. In most cases you can manage that as well as anyone else. You don't have to spend hundreds of dollars to hire a specialist or to be trained in the procedures to follow. It's a relatively simple matter of determining what your credit files say about you and then following through to set the record straight, assert your legal rights, or negotiate a settlement of an outstanding debt *on terms you can manage* in exchange for a restored good credit rating.

You can do it. You don't have to be a victim of the system. You *can* make the system work for you.

Here's how.

1

Establishing Credit

It would be nice if when you needed money a friendly person would come to your door, hand you $5,000, and say, "Pay me back when you can." Most people, out of conscience and appreciation, would be sure to repay the loan.

But for the average person life isn't that friendly or convenient. We have to depend on credit from banks or retailers to ease us through times when we're short of cash for the goods or services we need. And the reality is that those who provide credit are more interested in making a profit from us than in just helping us out. They're not as concerned with our need as they are with whether we'll make the payments due under terms of whatever credit agreement is arranged. They don't care that we have a need; they just want to know that they'll get back any money loaned to us under the agreement—plus interest, of course.

How do they make that determination? When it comes to loans or bank charge cards, it's commonly through impersonal assessment of responses to a series of standard questions on an application form. The answers are assigned a point value and weighted according to creditors' experience of financial stability within the public at large. In order for the desired credit to be granted, the person applying has to "score" at least a given number of points in the answers given.

A credit scoring guideline currently in widespread use weights responses as follows:

Marital Status
Married	1
Single	0

Residence
Rent	1
Own with mortgage	4
Own w/out mortgage	3
Any other	0

Dependents
1 to 3	1
Over 3	0
None	0

Age
21 to 25	0
26 to 64	1
65 and over	0

Previous Residence
0 to 5 years	0
6 years and over	1

Employment
Less than 1 year	0
1 to 3 years	1

| 4 to 6 years | 2 |
| Over 7 years | 3 |

Monthly Income

Up to $600	1
$600 to $800	2
$800 to $1000	4
Over $1000	6

Monthly Obligations

| $0 to $200 | 1 |
| Over $200 | 0 |

Occupation

Unskilled	1
Skilled	2
Professional	3

Credit History

| Loan with bank | 4 |
| Other loans | 2 |

The minimum qualifying point total on this application is 18. If your answers add up to less than this number, your application will be denied. Character is nowhere taken into account. Ironically, a person who lies on his or her application in order to make the point cutoff may be granted credit while the application from an honest person of good character is denied.

Whenever you fill out a credit application, treat it as you would a test, because it *is* a test. Your score determines whether your request will be approved or denied. Be sure to respond to each question. If there's a question that doesn't apply to you, write "n/a" (not applicable) on that line. Type in the information or print neatly; many sloppy applications go straight into a trash basket because the reviewer can't read them.

And always make a master copy of the application to keep in your own files for reference when filling out others.

Credit applications also commonly ask for other credit references. Be sure to list any cards you have, even if you are in arrears on one or another account. These will appear on your credit records, anyway, and you don't want to arouse suspicion that you are trying to hide something.

But then we come back to this question: How do you establish credit if you have no credit history and the point value of your answers on a credit application falls below the cutoff line?

Well, you may not be able to swing a bank loan, but there are credit options open to you. Perhaps the easiest way to establish credit on a first-time basis is to go to a department store, put clothes or some other item on a layaway plan, and pay for the purchase over time. Do this for a year, then go to the store manager and ask for an application for a store card. The store will check on your layaway plan payment history, see that you have a good payment record, and thus should be willing to open a charge account in your name. (Let the store manager know you are doing this to establish credit. That will be in your favor.)

You see, for the first-time applicant, the key is to show *responsibility*. Show a potential creditor that you are conscientious in paying off debts and you have a good chance of being granted credit.

One device being promoted by banks as a means of establishing good credit is the "secured" bank charge card (MasterCard or Visa). You apply to the bank for the card; the bank requires you to make a security deposit, which may range from $250 to $1,000, to cover them against any risk that you may fail to make payments. Further, your initial credit limit will be kept low in comparison to that granted customers the bank has decided are a good credit risk, who will be issued cards without any security deposit requirement. It's a good deal for the bank, because they'll be earning money with your security deposit, as well as on the card itself.

A secured bank charge card may help you establish credit, but don't be fooled into thinking it's a cure for bad credit. A lot of people make that mistake. Other creditors will know the bank has covered itself against any potential losses. They'll review your overall credit record and make their decisions according to that. If there's a bad payment record or an indication of default, they'll count the risk of losing any of their money as too high. Even if there are no bad marks against you, because you have no previous credit record at all, don't expect other creditors immediately to decide you're a good credit risk because now the bank has issued you a secured card. It's not just having the card that counts; it's building a consistent record of reliable payments. Again, you have to prove your responsibility.

Taking out a secured loan—that is, one backed up by a stated asset sufficient to cover any money owed in the event of default—is another route to establishing credit. Pledge a certificate of deposit or a passbook account as collateral. If you don't have the necessary assets, arrange a loan from a family member or friend. Put the money into a CD or passbook account that you'll pledge as collateral for the bank loan. When you get the money from the bank, use it to pay back the family member or friend. Then be scrupulous in following the payment schedule for the bank loan; once it's paid in full, you'll have a favorable, established

credit record (provided you have no history of poor performance in any other credit matter).

Note that arranging a secured loan via use of funds
borrowed from a family member or friend means the
money you get through the loan is immediately spo-
ken for. Repay the private loan; don't renege on an
agreement to reimburse the person promptly because
you want to use the money for a preferred personal
objective. You'll only wind up with two debts to deal
with. You don't want an arrangement designed to
prove you can handle credit responsibly to complicate
your finances immediately.

You may not find it easy to get the kind of credit
you want right when you want it, but sooner or later
you'll have it. Credit is like anything else—if you want
it bad enough, eventually you'll get it. And because
there's profit in granting credit, creditors want to extend it to as many people as possible—as long as these
people appear responsible.

While establishing it may seem a terrible problem
to young people just beginning a career and impatient
for the benefits credit provides, the real problems arise
later. You become dependent on it to establish and
maintain your life-style, then suddenly discover that
for some reason you can't live up to the demands of
all your creditors. You find those demands are loud
and insistent, with little thought given to any difficulties you may be having. It's pay what you owe or risk
losing everything you have and then being consigned
to virtual economic imprisonment.

You miss some payments, and even though there's
no question of dishonest intent on your part, you wind
up with a black mark on your credit record. And from
that point on you're effectively blackballed by creditors, treated as someone who is not responsible and

excluded from any future economic transaction that involves credit. That can mean problems purchasing needed big-expense items, maintaining your home in good repair, underwriting the security of your family, even establishing a home of your own.

How did you get yourself into this mess? What do you do now?

2

The Credit Card Merry-Go-Round

You're a married couple who have demonstrated sufficient financial stability and responsibility to assure creditors that you are a good credit risk. The husband is steady at his job (which means he's been at his job for at least three years). You have good credit at two department stores. You've purchased a home, with a nice down payment and the benefit of a mortgage issued by a local bank, and you're grateful to the bank for giving you the mortgage.

You don't stop to ask yourself who was doing whom the favor in arranging the mortgage. You don't compare who's risking what: The bank has your home as collateral. If you can't make your payments, the bank doesn't really lose; you lose, and what you lose is your home! The bank doesn't have any qualms of conscience. You'd be irresponsible in not making your mortgage payments. It wouldn't make a difference to them if the family wage earner was laid off or injured on the job and unable to work anymore. Something like that isn't their problem, it's yours.

But it hasn't come to that yet. You're in your home— paying the mortgage and handling the living expenses on one salary—and just managing.

Then a miracle happens. You receive a credit card application in the mail because you're a homeowner. Wait, here's another. Two different institutions are inviting you to apply for credit, and it's clear on both applications that you've already been approved. Wow! You fill out the applications, in both your and your spouse's names, then mail them back, thinking, "This is the answer to our needs. Now we can get some of the things we need without running through our whole paycheck each week."

A couple weeks go by and you receive the two credit cards. You're as excited as if someone had made you a present of all the things you can now afford to buy. Now you can buy that $600 television-VCR combination you've been wanting but couldn't afford before. Sure, you have to pay for it eventually, but that won't be a problem. You don't have to pay for it all at once. You pay in modest installments you can afford, with a little interest added on. Meanwhile you're finally enjoying a little more of the good life you've worked so hard for. You've really earned it, you tell yourself.

Your first credit card has a $1,000 credit limit, which means you have $400 left in credit after charging $600 for the TV and VCR on this card. And you have another $1,000 credit on the other card. No problem here. You get paid every week. You've been told the interest charges amount to 19% a year, but that doesn't register in terms of a significant amount of money. As long as the payments are comfortably low.

Thirty days later your first bill comes in the mail.

It states, "Pay either $600 or $24." Naturally you pay the $24 and you still have your TV and VCR. Hey, what's $24? This is a piece of cake!

Then another miracle happens—a baby is coming into your life. This means more needs, but you're not so much worried as excited by this wonderful new development. You have to get baby furniture, maternity clothes, clothes for the baby, extra food, etc., but thank God, you've got credit cards. They'll make the added expenses manageable, just as when purchasing the TV and VCR.

So you take the second credit card and charge $800 on it. That still leaves you $200 credit on this card, plus you've got $400 credit on the first card. You realize you're limited now, so you resolve to be very careful in how you use those cards from now on.

Unfortunately, when the bills come in thirty days later, you discover you're already up against a bit of a problem. Now you have to pay $24 on the first card plus $48 on the second, for a total of $72 a month beyond what you're spending on routine household expenses plus mortgage payments. But you didn't have that kind of monthly surplus to begin with. That one paycheck just managed to cover the necessities.

You manage somehow. Then you decide to make life a little easier and get an oil company credit card to pay for your gasoline. After all, you need the gas, anyway. But now you wind up tanking up for $15 a week instead of putting in $5 worth at a time, as you did when paying cash. And at the end of the month you've got a $60 gasoline bill to take care of. That's in addition to the $72 you have to scratch together to cover the minimum payments on your other credit cards. And it's not as if you've been putting money aside in a cookie jar—that paycheck seems to run out just as fast as it ever did. You ask yourself, "How did we get into this mess?"

Somehow you still manage to pay each bill on time, and at least now you have everything you wanted. Well, there is this or that other thing you really want or need and can get on credit, so you do. And then you're at your credit limit and can't charge anymore. But you still have to pay the bills each month. Now you're not receiving any new items, just making burdensome payments.

It's an uncomfortable, threatening situation. All your money is going toward bills, more than ever before, and you've no way to buy some of the things you need but have had to put off—new clothes, a new washer to replace the one that's broken down.

Then you figure a way to keep up with your needs. You apply for another card and think this will do it. But all you're doing is digging yourself deeper and deeper into debt, thanks to credit card charge privileges. And you discover that even though you keep paying on the charges you've run up—and paying rather a lot!—the balance isn't going down. You find yourself running faster and faster in an effort to keep up with the monthly payments, but it feels like you're falling behind just the same.

You take a hard look at what's happening, and for the first time you realize the impact of those high interest rates you are paying, something you didn't really pay attention to when you first received those cards. You were happy then; everything seemed so easily manageable—a simple minimum payment every month that didn't amount to all that much. But here you are, less than a year later, and that simple minimum somehow grew into a big headache, with a $30 to $35 charge added in each month for interest. Your paycheck is stretched to the absolute limit just making payments, and you're not receiving any new merchandise. You slack off on your payments. Some months they go in a day or two late; some months they're a week or more late.

And then you have a household crisis. You have no choice but to use the money you have on hand, which means there's no money at the end of the month to pay those credit bills. So for one month you don't pay. You make the payment the subsequent month, thinking at least you are paying. You don't realize the effect that month of nonpayment has on your credit record, but that's of no concern at the moment. Except then you decide to get another card for the things you need to buy but don't have the cash for, and you're turned down because of bad credit.

At first you hang loose and just accept the denial, telling yourself, "Oh well, I basically have everything." But before long you feel the pinch of not being able to get something you really need, and then you get mad. "Who are they to do this to me?" you ask yourself, and you get so mad you stop paying your credit bills altogether. This leads to hassles with the banks and stores, but you decide you don't care, because you can't buy anything else, anyway, and still have all the merchandise you bought on credit. Not only do you not pay your credit card bills, but you feel perfectly justified in refusing to do so—after all, the creditors don't care what happens to you!

You go through life with this attitude for years. As far as you're concerned, you refused to participate any longer in a big rip-off. In your mind you owe nobody.

Five years go by, and once again you're living from paycheck to paycheck. The only change is in the world around you—the neighborhood is going downhill and it's time to move for the children's sake. That means you have to face up to some harsh realities. Well, you're older. You know what's right. You're ready to demonstrate responsibility again but find yourself "locked in" your old home in a deteriorating neighborhood. Why? Because as a result of bad credit performance in years past you can't get a mortgage for a new home.

You find yourself in a panic. If you have to, you'll pay to have the situation corrected, to restore your credit. You'll cough up whatever fee is necessary to someone who can advise you on how to clean up your credit record.

This is a typical scenario with millions of people who get caught up on the credit card merry-go-round, not understanding what they're getting into by running up credit charges. It's just that they want more than simply to survive, and credit cards tantalize with the promise of the good life within easy, affordable reach—a seemingly modest monthly payment can get you whatever you might happen to want or need. If the rich can do it, why not anyone?

The skeptical, practical-minded person may very well decide that the solution is to avoid credit cards altogether. Pay cash for everything. If you don't have the cash to pay for merchandise, then you can't afford it. It's as simple as that, and that will keep you out of any difficulty.

But it really isn't that simple. In this day and age, sooner or later virtually everyone needs to borrow money—for most people it's impossible to wait to buy a new car or a home until they've accumulated enough cash to do so. So at one point or other they'll be applying for a loan. Then they find that refusing to establish credit through the usual consumer channels means they have no credit, and no credit is the same as bad credit. In order to establish a credit record, they have to get a credit card.

Credit cards are an unavoidable fact of life for most people in today's economy. Moreover, they do provide the benefit of convenience, making purchases possible that might otherwise be hard to manage. But they come with a price attached, a price that often isn't immediately clear to those seduced by the convenience they offer. Too often a consumer wakes up belatedly to the fact that he's caught on the credit card merry-go-round. The round of payments keeps accelerating, and the only escape he sees is simply to jump off this crazy carousel, refusing to keep up with the payments that threaten eventually to destroy him.

This is how one out of every ten credit card holders gets into trouble, because as soon as you stop payment on these debts, a black mark is entered on your credit records. From then on, you'll be treated like a marked man (or woman), locked out of the credit system, locked into a world of limited economic opportunity. And until you can clear your record, that's where you'll stay.

3

Credit Bureaus, Credit Reports, and Your Credit Rating

From the first time you participate in a transaction involving credit, you have a credit record. And this isn't just an abstract something, it's an actual dossier kept on you, recording the particulars of the credit you've applied for, any credit you've been granted, and your credit performance. In effect, as soon as you've introduced yourself to the credit system, Big Brother starts watching you.

Big Brother, in this case, takes the form of a credit bureau, a central clearinghouse with huge computer banks that store information on you forwarded by creditors you've established relations with. The credit bureau also responds to and records credit inquiries from potential creditors interested in lining you up as one of their customers. An extensive file gradually builds up without any direct input from you—a file with far-reaching power over your economic future.

A credit bureau is a subscriber service for any of a range of creditors—banks, merchants, insurance agen-

cies, etc.—who have or anticipate any arrangement involving a regular schedule of payments to be made by
a consumer for desired or needed goods and services.
There are six major credit reporting services in the
United States, and 98 percent of all credit bureaus in
the country are either owned outright or affiliated with
these companies. Together they control more of our
lives than most people realize, and yet the public has
hardly any sense of who they are.

The largest credit reporting service is a company
called TRW, with headquarters in Orange, California.
TRW keeps files on at least 180 million Americans.
The second largest, Trans Union, with headquarters
in Chicago, has at least 150 million Americans on file.
The third largest is Chilton Automatic Systems, located in Dallas. The fourth, Credit Bureau Corporation, has its headquarters in Atlanta and provides
equifax (telecommunications) service systems that
banks use for keeping track of customers' credit performance. Pinger System, in Houston, does not oper-
ate in as wide an area as the others because it is more
conservative in its business practices. Leascore, in
Philadelphia, specializes in the credit performance of
individuals or companies renting or leasing property.
(The home address for each bureau appears in Appendix 1.)

If you've ever applied for credit, you can bet one or
more of these companies has your name on file. And
the information listed in your file, which is issued as
a credit report to subscribers asking about your credit
history, can make the difference between economic
freedom and economic imprisonment.

Three different parties have access to your credit
records—the credit bureau itself, any subscribing creditor, and you. The fact that you are guaranteed access

by law means that you also have a certain amount of
control. You're entitled to see the information held on
you and to demand changes in the record to correct
inaccuracies or bring it up to date. This is important,
because it's very common for credit records to contain
inaccuracies or carry information that is legally out-
dated and may not properly be used against you.
That's why I recommend you take the time to find out
what is on your report *before* you apply for any credit
arrangement on a needed service or purchase. You
could well discover something that discredits you; you
might be able to remedy that before your application
is processed and denied—and it will be, if a questionable point isn't somehow cleared off the record.

Your credit report is divided into five sections. The
first section is the Identification portion, which already offers possibilities for error that may affect the
accuracy of the rest of your records. It's essential that
the name, birthdate, address, Social Security number,
and employment history given for you are correct. (In
some cases a telephone number is also given.) These
are the ID tags used by the bureau to enter details
into your credit record. You want to be sure your identification particulars aren't misstated in such a way
that credit information not pertaining to you winds up
in your file.

Following the Identification section of the report is
your Credit History. This includes the name and identification number of subscribers and creditors who now
have or have had a credit relationship with you. The
creditors will have indicated your payment pattern, in
particular whether your account is kept current or you
fall behind in your payments—by thirty days, sixty
days, ninety days, or longer. They also will have indicated the date the account was opened, the original

balance or credit limit, and the terms of the credit arrangement. For example, if you see "12 × 120" indicated next to mention of a bank loan, that means payments of $120 to be made over a twelve-month period.

The next section is Credit Inquiries, listing every time a subscriber or creditor pulls a credit report on you with your permission. Each time this kind of request comes in, the computer automatically records the "inquiry." The count of inquiries can remain on your record for as long as two years. This may seem an innocent enough list of entries, but, as we'll see shortly, it can actually be used against you as a sign of bad credit.

The section that follows Credit Inquiries is Public Records. Credit bureaus have access to the public records from any courthouse, and what they find there with your name on it is also used to determine your creditworthiness. If someone has sued you and the case has been recorded in the public records with a docket number, notice of the suit will show up on your credit report for any subscriber to see. You can bet that will affect your credit rating, and not favorably.

The last part of the report—and vitally important to you—is the section headed Consumer Statement. Most consumers are unaware that they have the right to enter a statement of up to one hundred words regarding any account they wish to clarify, notably an account that is being disputed. Remember, the credit history given for you comes entirely from your creditors, and the credit bureau almost always takes their word for gospel when it comes to your account records. The reality is that mistakes are sometimes made, introducing error into your credit record. You wind up being reported as a bad credit risk when in fact you've always dealt responsibly with the creditor involved. Or an account continues to be marked delinquent after you've cleared it, and that, too, results in your being rated a poor credit risk. The Consumer Statement lets you alert other creditors that there's a question as to the accuracy of a given account summary.

Keep in mind that not all of your accounts will be reported to all the credit bureaus. Some creditors subscribe to one bureau but not another, so the relevant account information will appear in one bureau's credit report but not the other's. So when applying for credit, ask which credit bureau the creditor you are approaching uses. Then you can request a copy of that bureau's credit report, see what information they hold on you, and get a more accurate sense of whether your application is likely to be approved or denied.

It also helps to know which class of subscribers a particular creditor belongs to. There are two: limited subscribers and automatic subscribers. Limited subscribers report on your account only periodically, say once a month or even once every few months. Automatic subscribers have a direct computer connection, and any activity on your account immediately enters into the credit bureau's records. This direct connection generally results in a better record of accuracy. Limited subscribers are more likely to make mistakes in summarizing your account periodically, particularly with respect to keeping the record up-to-date. And because they make new entries into the record more slowly, it will generally take them longer to correct the record when it is in error.

How do you know which is which? By a code next to the creditor's name. When you see a TRW credit report, for example, there is an *A* or *M* code in the far left column next to the subscriber's name. *A* is for "automatic"; *M* is for "manual," or limited subscriber. Once you understand the distinction, you'll have a better sense of who is making mistakes on you and whether you can expect immediate correction or will have to anticipate some delay in that.

Now, the fact that you have the right of access to your credit record doesn't mean the credit bureau has to send you an immediate credit report the minute you ask for one. And it doesn't mean you can get it for free.

In order to receive a free credit report, you must have been denied credit *in writing* by a creditor. When you are denied credit in writing, the creditor must indicate in the denial letter which credit bureau provided the determining information. You must request the report within thirty days of the date of the denial letter. (If you wait more than thirty days, the credit bureau will charge you.) Then the credit bureau has thirty days to get back to you.

If you haven't actually been denied credit but want to see a copy of your credit report, anyway, you have that right, but you will have to pay a fee to get the report.

Having a copy of your credit report doesn't mean you'll immediately have all you need to resolve a bad credit situation. It's a necessary step in correcting any mistakes that appear on the record, of course, but your credit rating isn't only a matter of correcting mistakes and settling disputed accounts. There's still the matter of creditors' making a subjective determination that you're responsible, a good credit risk. Sometimes that determination seems very arbitrary indeed.

Strange as it seems, it's possible to be denied further credit when your past credit performance has been nothing short of exemplary. You may not get a loan because of "too much credit." Without any allowance made for your model payments record, a bank decides you can't be trusted with more credit. Or maybe the Credit Inquiries section of your credit report shows too many inquiries from potential creditors. "Too many inquiries"—more than six in the space of a year—means you're a bad credit risk, again no matter what your past performance record. Perhaps you bought an expensive home and have lived in it for a year with good credit. The bank will figure you don't have enough equity in your home yet to warrant extending you additional credit. (But let ten years go by in this same home and every bank will be at your door offering to lend you money.)

These credit denials are all made on the basis of information in your credit report. Sadly, you can be denied needed credit even when you've done nothing to mark you as irresponsible and your credit report is free of any error you can dispute. You're not regarded as innocent until you've actually messed up. Instead, you're as good as guilty, and without a fiscal sin on your conscience.

It can be even worse if you've ever gotten into trouble in a credit arrangement, later take steps to clear your account, and then blindly trust the creditor to erase the black mark on your record. I know a woman who had failed to make payment on a $600 bill from a department store. That failure, of course, was entered on her record. Fortunately, fate was kind and her fortunes changed for the better. She decided to clear her record; she had learned from her mistakes how to control money. She contacted the store and was told simply to pay the amount owed. She did so, assuming this would automatically clear her record. Imagine her distress to learn that her previous bad payments record continued to appear in her credit report. The store, the party responsible for updating the record, made no effort to notify the credit bureau of the changed situation. Adding insult to injury, the store also turned down her new credit application, because of her past (outdated) record. And yet another person owing the same store a similar amount was able to get her credit records updated and her credit rating upgraded once her debt was paid. In that case the store cooperated.

That's how arbitrary and erratic the system can be. This is how it all too often works, continuing the victimization of people who have in fact shown good faith and a readiness to accept financial responsibility. Is that really fair? I think that anyone who wants to correct his or her credit status should have the right to do so, just as anyone who has been sentenced for a crime is set free after serving his or her time.

You do, in fact, have rights in this respect. There are laws protecting you, but people are either ignorant of those laws or convince themselves they can't prevail against the overwhelming economic muscle of the credit system. It's unfortunately true that creditors often do behave as if they are above the law. For example, you are legally protected against harassment from companies seeking to collect on an overdue bill, and yet harassment by collection agencies remains a common practice. There are legal limits on how long a bad-debt entry may be carried on your credit records, and yet such entries often appear years after they ought to have been expunged.

I'm not saying people shouldn't pay their bills. I'm simply saying people shouldn't unnecessarily be victimized by a system that contrives deliberately to keep them in the dark while controlling much of their economic fortune. If people had a better sense of how the system works, they'd have a better chance of resolving their financial difficulties intelligently, with less risk of being consigned to a permanent second-class economic existence.

There would also be an improved chance of eliminating some of the continuing unfairness allowed in the system. Take the situation of a bill that carries a late payment charge. Suppose you are late by only two days, paying on the third instead of the first of the month. Typically your credit report will state that you are thirty days in arrears, not just two. The charge gets carried to the next billing cycle, and your credit rating suffers accordingly. If consumers were more active in monitoring their own credit records and the activity of the Big Brother credit bureaus, we'd be a far step further toward a more equitable system that gave the consumer equal status with the creditor.

4

How to Remedy a Poor Credit Rating

If you have any question about your credit rating, the first thing to do is get a copy of your credit report. That's the quickest, best way to identify the source of any difficulty you may be experiencing in connection with applying for or continuing a particular credit arrangement. In fact, given the importance of credit to full participation in contemporary society, I think it's a good idea to receive a copy of your credit report every six months or so to see how things stand.

If you've been denied credit, you will get a denial letter from the creditor, and the name and address of the reporting credit bureau will appear at the bottom of that letter. Make a copy of the denial letter to send to the credit bureau. (Keep a copy safely in your own files for backup in the event the other gets lost in the mail.) Include with the denial letter a letter from you requesting a free copy of your credit report, noting that you're responding within thirty days of the date of the denial letter. Be sure you clearly print or type your full name, address, Social Security number, and birth-date, as these are the ID tags used to pull the correct record. (Sample letters that you can easily adapt to your use appear in Appendix 3.)

If you haven't been denied credit but want a copy of your credit report, anyway, find out from a targeted creditor which credit bureau they subscribe to, then address your request accordingly. You will have to send along a fee with your request—call the credit bureau to find out what that is. Again, be sure you identify yourself fully, as above, and keep a copy of both your letter of request and the check or money order you've included with it. If you haven't received a reply after thirty days, write a follow-up letter, including with it a copy of your earlier request and payment.

When you receive your report—it may take as long as thirty days, and sometimes longer—review it carefully for accuracy.

Is your name given correctly? Are your address, Social Security number, and birthdate correct?

The Credit History section is particularly important. More credit problems are registered there than anywhere else, so it's important you take time to understand the information that appears there. (You will find a listing of codes and definitions on the back of your report to help you. Check the codes with your ratings to see where you stand and what codes have been applied to you. Subscriber codes identify creditors you have contacted or with whom you have established accounts.)

Review the accounts listed on the report. Are they all yours?

If an account that is not yours appears on the list, you already have cause for dispute. Immediately notify the credit bureau that they have incorrectly listed an account that is not yours on your report. Ask them to investigate this account and to respond with a corrected credit report within thirty days, reserving the right to dispute any inaccuracies that may appear there. (Every notification should be in writing, with your full name, address, Social Security number, and birthdate given clearly in each communication. Use of certified mail is advised, and keep copies of *all* correspondence for backup in your own files.)

In your Credit History you will see creditors listed, together with notes on terms of your credit agreement. A column to the right contains a row of X's. These indicate your payments pattern. If the X's run straight across without interruption, that means you are paying your bill promptly each month. Interruptions in the row indicate interruptions in payment. It only takes a glance for someone to determine how faithfully you make payments.

In the last column is a number indicating how the creditor—a store, bank, etc.—rates you for credit. The numbers range from R01 to R09, with R01 the most favorable rating. If anyone rates you R09—the worst rating you can get—you will get turned down on any further credit application, unless you take steps to upgrade that rating significantly. Numbers between R01 and R09 indicate you've fallen short of perfection—for example, been late on payments—and may or may not rule out your getting further credit. But as we've observed, even an uninterrupted series of R01 ratings doesn't absolutely ensure your getting additional credit when you want it.

When looking at your Credit History records, check to see the dates given for each account. The first will be the date the account was opened by you. There will also be a date given for the last activity on any ac-

count. If you have an overdue account listed on your
credit report, what is the date of your last payment?

The Fair Credit Reporting Act stipulates that a delinquent account may be kept on a credit report no
longer than seven years from the date of the last
transaction. After that it must be removed from your
record, even if the balance was never paid off. Unfortunately credit bureaus commonly pretend not to understand what this means, and they will try to tell you
that the "date of the last transaction" means the date
on which the balance due is finally paid off. Don't let
them fool you. If that's the response you get, write
them and insist they follow the terms of the law; include a copy of the law with your letter to show you
know your rights. (Sections of the Fair Credit Reporting Act are reproduced in Appendix 2.)

Don't worry that the creditor is being thrown for a
total loss on the amount due. The creditor will already
have written off the loss and received a tax credit.
When people pay off on accounts that are several years
overdue, a creditor can actually profit—receiving the
money owed and being allowed the previous tax write-
off, anyway. That's not to encourage nonpayment of
debts—you still cut yourself off from any credit options
during the seven-year period that a bad debt remains
on your record.

If it's been less than seven years since the date of
last activity on a past-due account that you've verified
as yours, you don't necessarily have to wait until seven
years have passed before you can repair your credit.
However, it will take action on the debt to achieve
your objective.

In this case your first step is to write to the creditor and propose a payment arrangement. Send a letter identifying yourself and the account in question

clearly, explaining that you have fallen behind in your payments and what the reasons are behind that—loss of a job, illness in the family, etc. Tell the creditor that you would like to reopen the account to reestablish your creditworthiness—you want to make payment on your debt.

If you have the full amount now, notify the creditor that you are prepared to pay in full, provided they agree to upgrade your credit rating accordingly, removing any reference to delinquency or poor performance on the account.

Just sending a letter to this effect isn't enough. You're really negotiating a contractual agreement— you want the letter including this proviso to have the effect of a contract between you and the creditor. To achieve that, ask the creditor to sign the letter itself as an indication of agreement and then mail it back to you. Tell them you will make your payment upon receipt of the signed letter. (A sample letter you can adapt for your use appears in Appendix 3.)

After you've received the letter back, signed by a representative of the creditor, and followed through on payment as promised, follow up with a check on your credit report. Allow at least ten days to give the credit bureau a chance to update the record, then write for the current report. If you find that the creditor has not cleared you on the account in question, write to them (the creditor, *not* the credit bureau) and demand that they do so within twenty-four hours or you will sue. Remember again to identify yourself and the account clearly. Include a copy of the agreement letter (keep the original in your own file) with this letter; send it by certified mail.

If you get no cooperation from the creditor at this point, go ahead and sue for whatever damages you suffered as a result of their failure to clear your credit rating.

We had a case where we sent a creditor of one of our clients an agreement letter that was subsequently sent back to us, signed by a representative of the company. We waited for the record on the account to be cleared, but nothing happened. So I contacted the creditor by phone. I told them they were obliged to clear our client's credit record because they had signed an agreement to do so. The company spokesperson told me someone in the office had signed the agreement letter as a joke, without telling anyone else about it. The joke was on them, I replied, because if action wasn't taken to clear the record, a lawsuit would follow. The creditor knew the client was within his rights and very quickly amended the record.

Suppose, however, that you cannot pay the bill in full but would still like to clear the record. What do you do then?

You follow a similar procedure, but take concrete steps to show your good faith before negotiating the contractual arrangement by which your credit record is cleared.

Write a letter explaining that you want to clear the bad debt off your record, that your financial difficulties have cleared to the point where you can begin doing so, and set up a schedule of monthly payments that you will follow. Then follow through conscientiously. After at least two or three payments on this account, write back to the creditor, asking them in good faith to upgrade your credit rating, pointing out that you're making payment as promised and feel restoration of a good credit rating is in order.

If the answer you get is no, don't give up. Continue with your payments and repeat your request until you get a positive acknowledgment. Keep in mind that a creditor won't immediately trust you as a paying customer again—first they've got to see consistent evidence of financial responsibility, and a few modest payments on what may be a big debt won't necessarily convince them you're serious. So continue your payments, with or without their explicitly approving your arrangement.

When you are down to an amount that you can pay off in full, send a letter of agreement for them to sign, offering now to pay the debt in full if they'll agree to clear your credit record fully. Remember, they still want your money, even if they've already written it off. Chances are excellent that you'll get their agreement. After all, in business it's the bottom line that counts.

Again, after you've won agreement and made your payment, be sure to follow up with a review of the account as reported in your credit report.

Obviously you've got to resolve any account problems that become apparent in a review of the Credit History section of your report. It's only logical that that's where you'd expect to find the reason for any credit difficulties you're experiencing. But don't omit looking through the rest of your credit report.

Check the Credit Inquiries list. Too many inquiries can result in denied credit, too, so it's wise to make sure that all inquiries listed are a result of applications you've put in. No company or institution may be listed among the inquiries if you never gave them permission to check your credit. (Signing a credit application is the usual way in which you grant permission.) If a company you've never granted permission is listed, write the credit bureau and insist on their removal from the list.

Is there anything in the Public Records section that might be having a negative effect on your credit record? Are the particulars of any entry inaccurate?

Also, take advantage of the Consumer Statement section. Are you disputing the accuracy of any account report? Are you holding up payment on a consumer debt because the item you bought or the service you asked for was not up to advertised standards? Have you been victimized by credit card fraud, with unauthorized purchases charged against your account and follow-up investigations so far inconclusive? Have you missed payments due to extraordinary circumstances but are taking measures to meet your obligations? Put it in the record. It could make the difference between someone reading you as creditworthy or as a poor credit risk.

Finally, consider the possibility of something outside your credit report resulting in the denial of a credit application. I was once denied a credit card and had difficulty figuring out what the problem was. So I called the company involved and asked why I'd been denied. It turned out I'd forgotten to put my ZIP code on the application. Most people, I suspect, would just have thrown up their hands in despair, assuming a problem with their credit rating and feeling powerless to do anything about it. It's because of this experience that I tell everyone, "If ever you're denied credit, follow up on it. Find out why." The problem may not be with your credit rating at all.

On the other hand, if you find your credit rating is the problem, recognize that you can still do something about it. Get your credit report, pinpoint the problem, and then take the appropriate action to address the problem. You don't have to settle for being a victim of the system.

5

Collection Agencies, You, and the Law

The phone rings, and immediately you feel tense. You've been getting upsetting calls lately and fear this is another one—a call from a collection agency dunning you for payment of an overdue debt. Why can't they understand that you just don't have the money right now? Why do they keep harassing you? You wish there were some way you could make them leave you alone.

This is an all too common scenario for people who have overextended themselves through use of credit and too late discovered themselves unable to satisfy their creditors. Lacking the means to make payment, they've fallen behind on their obligations. After receiving several notices from their creditors requesting immediate payment of the amount overdue, these people suddenly find themselves dealing with a new party—a collection agency. And frequently they find themselves pursued so aggressively that the question of settling their debts takes on an absolutely hellish

aspect. I've known the resultant pressures to drive
people to a nervous breakdown.

What exactly is a collection agency? How do they
get involved in the relationship between you and
a creditor? Are there any limits on the lengths to
which they can go in trying to make you pay your
debt?

A collection agency is simply a specialized business
agency set up to pursue payment on debts that a creditor has not been able to settle through standard
billing and notification procedures. Rather than as-
signing personnel to keep after a past-due account that
might still not be paid despite the extra effort, the
creditor turns it over to the collection agency. In effect, they hire an outside specialist who is specifically
oriented to the task at hand—making you pay what
you owe.

Naturally, the collection agency has an arrangement with the creditor to cover its own cost of doing
business. It may pay the creditor a percentage of the
debt owed—in effect, buy the debt at a discount—then
keep for itself whatever it manages to collect from you.
Or it may work on a commission basis, claiming a percent of whatever money is collected on behalf of the
creditor and forwarding the balance to the creditor. In
either case the agency's ability to make money as a
business depends entirely on its collection success rate.
So it's not surprising to find a repertoire of aggressive
techniques being used to pressure consumers into paying up what they owe, never mind what hardships may
be behind a particular failure to pay.

The good news is that there are legal controls on
the lengths to which a collection agency can go in its
efforts to push you into paying off a bad debt. These
controls are spelled out in the Fair Debt Collection

Practices Act, passed by Congress specifically to reduce collection agency harassment of consumers. Congress had come to the realization that too many
consumers, desperate to end such harassment, were
declaring bankruptcy to get relief. And that was in
nobody's best interests. So now there are clear legal
controls on the measures to which a collection agency
or an attorney who collect debts on a regular basis
may go to push you to a payment of personal, family,
or household debts—including money owed on a car
loan, for medical care, or for charge accounts.

- Are you getting calls from a collection agency
  before eight A.M. or after nine P.M.? Are you being addressed in an abusive manner?

- Are you getting calls at work? Have you been
  embarrassed or threatened with embarrassment
  on the job?

- Has a collection agent contacted family members
  or neighbors about your debt?

- Is a collector calling you repeatedly, despite your
  request to leave you alone?

- Have you been threatened with arrest if you
  don't pay your bill?

If the answer to any of these questions is yes, the
collection agency is in violation of the Fair Debt Collection Practices Act. You don't have to put up with
any of this!

So why are people routinely subjected to this kind
of treatment? The answer is easy—and unfortunate:
Most people don't realize they have rights in this area.
They assume the law is entirely on the creditors' side.
Collection agencies know this and count on consumer

timidity to keep people from asserting their rights. In fact, agency training programs still regularly include tactics on how to intimidate debtors into paying their bills.

Don't let yourself be intimidated! Assert your rights in any dealings with a collection agency.

Under the terms of the Fair Debt Collection Practices Act, you can actually stop collectors from contacting you simply by writing a letter telling them to stop. (Send it by certified mail.) After that they may not legally contact you again except to let you know that some specific action is to be taken by them or the creditor to recover what you owe. That, of course, would be an action through the courts.

If you have an attorney, the Fair Debt Collection Practices Act states that the collector may not contact anyone but the attorney. If you do not have an attorney, the collector may contact other people only to find out where you live or work. The agency may not tell those people about your debt, and as a rule no person may be contacted more than once, even for limited informational purposes.

But, of course, a collector does have the right to contact you at least once to follow up on a debt owed. And that contact may be repeated within reasonable limits until such time as you write a letter formally requesting contact be discontinued or refer the matter to your attorney.

When you receive a call from an agency, immediately ask for the name of the person speaking to you. Make a note of it. In fact, keep a log of every call—the date and time of the call, the agency name, who spoke to you, what that person told you and in what manner, and how you responded. Let the collection agent know you're keeping a log of the calls.

If the collection agent speaks in a threatening or abusive manner, don't panic. Stay cool. Inform the agent quietly that you know your rights and that you will file a complaint in response to any abusive or harassing behavior on the part of the agency.

If that's not enough to keep you from being harassed, the thing to do is write a formal letter of complaint to the Federal Trade Commission. Give the collection agency's name, address, and telephone number. Then provide the details of how you were or are being harassed: who spoke to you, the dates and times of each call, and the nature of the conversation. Be sure you provide whatever information you have on any third-party calls the collection agency may have made disclosing your debt—to family members, neighbors, or your employer. Close your letter of complaint with a request that the FTC take steps to investigate and eliminate the unfair practices to which you are being subjected. (See the sample letter in Appendix 3.)

Send a copy of the letter to both the creditor for whom the collection agency is acting and the collection agency itself. The creditor should prove sensitive to association with any unfair business practices that may reflect unfavorably on them. And since the last thing a collection agency wants is a state or federal investigation of their collection practices, they are likely to cease their objectionable practices promptly.

As with all such correspondence, be sure to keep a copy for your files. That way, if you get no response and the harassment continues, you can send a second letter including all the particulars of the first. You can also send a letter to the Attorney General's office, putting on record a complaint that the collection agency has violated federal law as spelled out in the Fair Debt Collection Practices Act.

If the actions of the collection agency have caused you severe damage—for example, created such emotional strain that you are having a hard time functioning normally or resulted in your getting fired—contact your attorney as well and file a lawsuit right away.

A collection agency found guilty of unfair debt collection practices can be fined up to $10,000 for each instance of such practice. Agency personnel acting in a harassing fashion risk the loss of their jobs. And you can still collect in a suit for personal damages suffered at the hands of either the agency or its personnel.

The truth is, you're not even obliged to deal with the collection agency when it comes to trying to clear a debt. You can deal directly with the creditor—after all, that's who you owe. If the agency "bought" the debt at a discount, any adjustment to be made will have to be between them and the creditor. You're not bound by their arrangement.

Contact the responsible person at the creditor's office and tell him or her that you want to clear away your debt. You've suffered a recent financial setback but want to show good faith in paying off your obligation. Tell them you are prepared to work out a payment agreement to get back in their good graces. If they propose payment installments that are beyond your means, let them know you can't afford payments that high—taking on more than you could handle is what got you into trouble in the first place. Tell them you are budgeting your money and stipulate what amount you can afford.

The procedure here is the same as I've already de-

tailed in Chapter 4. Seal the arrangement you negotiate with a letter of agreement that you ask the
creditor's authorized representative to sign; address
the letter directly to the person to whom you spoke.
Be certain that your agreement clearly states that as
your debt is paid off, your credit rating will be ad-
justed accordingly. (If you forget to do that, you may
find yourself with a balance of $0 owed but a credit
rating of R-09 just the same.)

When it comes to unsecured debt—that is, financial
obligations that do not involve your putting up collateral against the possible eventuality of default—
creditors would generally rather negotiate a workable
arrangement for repayment than risk not receiving
their money at all. Of course, you should recognize
that they will first press for immediate or prompt payment of the total amount due. However, once you make
it clear that that is impossible—you can't pay money
you don't have—and that you are acting in good faith,
they will usually prove amenable to an alternate arrangement.

Once you've negotiated a schedule of payments with
the creditor directly, your response to any call from
the collection agency is that you are dealing with the
creditor directly. Tell them they can verify that with
the authorized creditor representative who signed your
letter of agreement. If after that the agency continues
with its collection efforts, notify them that you will file
a complaint of harassment against them.

Obviously a creditor owed money has the right to
take measures to secure payment. But it doesn't follow that a creditor or a collection agency hired by the
creditor has the right to use any combination of dirty
tricks they can think of to pressure you into immediate payment of your debt, without any regard to what

your situation may be. You don't have to put up with
harassment. You have rights, too. And it's through
knowledgeable insistence on your rights that you can
put an end to the abuses you may suffer at the hands
of unscrupulous bill collectors.

6

Bankruptcy—The Option to Avoid

As we observed in the previous chapter, in years past consumers often resorted to filing for bankruptcy in order to put an end to harassment by collection agencies. Attorneys routinely advised clients that this was the only way out of debt problems. And even today, despite advances in consumer protection legislation in this area, many consumers still conclude that bankruptcy is the only realistic option when facing a mountain of debts they haven't got the money to pay. Some don't realize they can solve their credit problems with the help of laws designed to protect them. Others simply don't understand how badly they can be affected as a result of declaring bankruptcy.

Let me spell it out plainly for you: Bankruptcy is not a quick or easy solution to any consumer's credit problems. In fact, bankruptcy is the worst thing that can appear on your credit record.

There are three types of bankruptcy, spelled out

in different chapters of the Federal Bankruptcy Act.

Chapter 7 (straight) bankruptcy is virtually a total wipeout of personal debts and assets. Everything you own, short of a few personal basics, is sold, and the proceeds are used to pay off your creditors. Needless to say, there are never enough assets to cover all the outstanding debts—if there were, you wouldn't need to go bankrupt—so the creditors usually wind up losing a substantial part of the money owed to them. Meanwhile there are still significant obligations that you're not allowed to discharge under this plan—notably, federal income tax owed, alimony, and child support payments.

The fact that you've declared bankruptcy is, naturally, entered into your credit record. A Chapter 7 filing stays on the record for as long as ten years, effectively labeling you an economic outcast when it comes to any further credit arrangement. You may not owe creditors any more payments on outstanding debt, but you'll be flat broke and no one will even consider lending you money or extending you credit so that you can get back on your feet financially. Meanwhile you're still faced with daily living expenses for you and your family—housing, food, clothing, transportation, medical needs, etc.

Perhaps you'll be able to manage on whatever income you have, but you'd better pray nothing goes wrong. Because if the unpaid bills start to pile up again, you can't erase them by filing for bankruptcy a second time. A minimum of six years must pass before you're allowed to file for another bankruptcy in the event of subsequent debt problems.

Considering the long-term effects of declaring straight bankruptcy under Chapter 7, you're far better off trying some other approach to eliminating your indebtedness. We've already highlighted one approach—negotiating payment agreements directly with creditors that are in line with what you can afford and gradually working down your debt that way. Your credit rating may be poor until you've achieved a zero balance, but at least you've got a chance of seeing your good rating restored once that's happened. You're not stuck with a black mark that stays on your record for ten years and consigns you to economic exile.

There is another bankruptcy option open to individuals—working out a Wage Earner Plan under Chapter 13 of the Federal Bankruptcy Act. This is a financial reorganization plan whereby you make up a payment plan to fit your budget and, under the supervision of the bankruptcy court, repay your creditors. (The court acts as a trustee.) Your payments must be adequate to pay off your creditors in three years or less, although occasionally the time period can be extended. You don't have to sell off your assets. In addition, the payment plan may also discount your debt—that is, you pay only a stipulated number of cents on each dollar owed.

To file for a Chapter 13 Wage Earner Plan, first you must go to the United States District Court in your area. There you will be given a form to fill out, listing your debts and income. Within one day a restraining order will go out to all of your creditors to stop legal action against you and prevent them from seizing any of your assets. The restraining order also prohibits collection agencies from contacting you on any matter and puts a halt to the further accumulation of all interest and late-payment penalties against you. Then a hearing is scheduled to work out the actual payment plan.

The fact that you have filed for a Chapter 13 Wage Earner Plan is entered on your credit report, and it stays there for seven years. While the loss of assets and the time period this fact stays on your record is not as great as with a straight Chapter 7 bankruptcy, this "blot" on your record may still affect your ability to arrange further credit. I have known some banks to issue mortgages to people who have filed under Chapter 13 only a couple of years after the filing, which indicates some open-mindedness about consumer difficulties here, but you can't count on this kind of understanding from every potential creditor.

The third bankruptcy option—filing under Chapter 11—is a business bankruptcy option and applies only to a business enterprise. (Under Chapter 11, a company is given protection from its creditors until it proposes a reorganization plan. That plan must be approved by creditor committees, and once that happens, the company can continue with business, even if some creditors have not been paid in full. Meanwhile the company can take drastic measures to ensure its survival, as long as the court trustee agrees these are warranted. Chapter 11 is the business alternative to filing for liquidation under Chapter 7, which companies as well as individuals may do. Note that if a business files for bankruptcy, it does not affect the credit standing of the owners or executives who ran it.)

Although creditors may not harass or threaten you to pressure you into paying your debts, they may take legal action to force payment. Often the debt owed by an individual is not enough to prompt legal action. Moreover, legal action can often push people into bankruptcy, and that hurts the creditor as well as the consumer.

But some creditors don't really care if they hurt themselves that way. They're satisfied because that's one less person they have to go after for payment—they can close the file and forget about it. I don't understand that kind of attitude myself. You would think they'd be patient and make an arrangement that eventually paid them the money owed.

I recommend that you avoid using bankruptcy as an escape from your debts—and especially avoid a Chapter 7 filing. Remember, declaring straight bankruptcy ruins your credit for the next ten years. Even if your credit report reflects a situation so grim that you can't see any way to clear the record in the foreseeable future, unpaid past-due accounts may be listed for no more than seven years. The slate is wiped clean—or should be, according to the law—three years sooner than if you declare straight bankruptcy. And there's always the possibility that your situation will improve and that you'll be able to negotiate a settlement with a creditor and raise your credit rating before seven years are up. You at least retain an element of control. With straight bankruptcy you are dead for years, with no control.

If you're pushed to the wall by a creditor's taking legal action against you and can't negotiate a payment plan, see if you can file under Chapter 13. That will remain fixed in the record for a full seven years and can also compromise your credit prospects significantly, but it may not block you from getting further credit through that whole period. Still, it will make things more difficult. Chapter 13 is a better solution to debt problems than Chapter 7, but not an option to reach for if it's at all avoidable.

Yes, it's your decision, and taking advantage of the bankruptcy laws is an available option. Your debts do get wiped out. But before you convince yourself that option spells "relief," look at the long-term implications. As a general rule, you're better off avoiding bankruptcy if that is at all possible.

7

Home Equity Loans—Beware!

Changes in the tax laws over the past several years have prompted banks and loan companies to come up with a new credit arrangement to the supposed benefit of consumers. You've seen and heard the advertisements everywhere—in newspapers, on television and radio. Consolidate all your outstanding debts into one that is more easily managed and allows you a tax deduction besides—take out a home equity loan. Use it to pay off what you owe on your charge cards, because now the interest on those isn't deductible. And the interest rate you'll be charged will be lower than that on your MasterCard, Visa card, or store charge card.

Wow! It makes so much sense, you almost feel you'd be stupid not to take advantage of this new credit option. You settle a pile of outstanding debts and now have just one monthly payment to deal with. You get a tax deduction and a break on the interest you've been paying. This is going to save you money. What have you got to lose?

Unfortunately a lot of people have learned the easy answer to that question the hard way. What you've got to lose is your home. And here's the really difficult question to answer: What will you do if that happens?

Let's look at the situation as it too commonly develops.

You find yourself on the credit card merry-go-round, with a load of debt that you're having more and more trouble keeping up with. You wish there were some way you could pay off all those accounts, get caught up and free of the pile of bills that descend on you every month. You can barely keep up with them, and a major chunk of every payment is just for interest. Somehow the balance due doesn't seem to drop from one month to the next. It would be so great to wipe the slate clean and start afresh.

And then one of those ads catches your eye: Mr./Ms. Homeowner, pay off those troublesome monthly bills with an easily arranged home equity loan. Quick approval, and then you have only one easy payment to deal with every month. And look, the interest is lower—and tax-deductible besides.

That's the solution, you decide. Here's a way to pay off the money you owe and get out from under that crushing burden of debt. You go to the bank, the loan officer goes over the loan application with you, confirms that you qualify for the loan, and there you are—you've got the money you need to retire outstanding debts, and all you had to do was fill out and sign a couple pieces of paper.

Now, suppose the amount you owe on various accounts totals $7,500. Do you take out a loan for $7,500? Well, no, you actually take out a loan for more than that. You include enough extra so that you'll have enough to make your first scheduled payment. Then there are a few home-maintenance/improvement needs you haven't been able to attend to up to now, so you also include enough extra to take care of those. You end up taking out a $10,000 home equity loan. You've reviewed the monthly payments for that size loan, and they're in line with what you feel you can afford.

And there you are. In the name of easing your debt burden, you've actually added to it. But you justify that by noting that the monthly payment on the loan really is manageable; you're not paying those high interest rates to which you were subjected before; and don't forget that tax deduction. Meanwhile you don't have those other bills to deal with. Your charge card balances have all been dropped to zero.

You live with the feeling of relief for a month or two—and then you notice something. You had to use your credit cards a couple of times to cover necessary purchases—gas for the car, new parts for the washer. So this month you have some credit card charges to pay off as well as making your monthly loan payment. You don't really have that much extra on hand after household expenses and the loan payment, so you make a partial payment. Yes, that leaves you with another bill to deal with next month, but it'll only be a little extra.

But next month there are a couple more items added to the credit card bill—other things you felt you needed. Same thing the next month . . . and the next month. Before you know it, your charge card debts are starting to mount up and you're stretched to your financial limit again, worrying how you're ever going to get caught up.

There's a serious illness in the family. An accident. A divorce. You're laid off. Or something else happens that unexpectedly hits you hard, right in the pocket-

book. You don't have a cash reserve to fall back on—
you wouldn't have needed a loan if you did. You can't
meet your monthly obligations, including the payment on your home equity loan. Now what?

Well, the credit card companies will notify you that
you're overdue on payments. If you don't pay the minimum due on the next bill, they'll freeze your account
and notify the credit bureau they report to that you're
delinquent. And there goes your credit rating.

The bank will notify you that you're overdue and, if
you don't promptly cough up what you owe, will move
to attach your home, since the papers you signed when
taking out the loan pledged your home as collateral.
You don't just lose your creditworthiness if you don't
keep up with your payments, you lose your house or
apartment. And don't expect that nice loan officer who
was so cooperative in helping you arrange this deal to
bear with you until you work yourself out of the difficult situation you're in.

How much better off are you now? The unsecured
credit debts you started off with may have been difficult to manage, but at least you still had your home.
Now you're facing a sheriff's sale—you agreed that if
you missed the payments on your loan the bank could
get their money back via the equity you have in your
home. And the way that happens is to force you to sell
your home, with no regard to market conditions and no
concern about where you and your family will end up.
If there's money left over after the bank debt and any
outstanding mortgage is paid, you'll get that, but it
won't be enough to replace your home. Depending on
your financial circumstances, it might not be enough
to rent a decent roof over your head.

Home equity loans are *not* a good deal for homeown-
ers who need extra money from somewhere to make

ends meet. While a loan may help you consolidate your debts, it really won't reduce them all that much. Certainly not enough to warrant the added risk you're taking. And then you're likely to be tempted to borrow just a bit extra to help tide you over.

Think about it. If you don't have ready cash reserves to fall back on, you're vulnerable to the first financial setback that hits you. Do you want your vulnerability stated in such a way that your home can be sold out from under you then?

If you're caught on the credit card merry-go-round, take steps to get off. Tighten your belt another notch and work those debts down with regular payments while holding off on further credit purchases. If you can't meet the minimum payments due, contact your creditor and try to negotiate a payment arrangement that you can manage. Don't compound your difficulties by putting your home explicitly at risk via a home equity loan. While you may be able to put off the day of reckoning that way, ultimately you still have to pay. And then, if anything goes wrong, the price will be devastating.

8

Choosing Your
Best Loan Option

Although I'm very conservative when it comes to telling anyone to take out a loan, at one time or another almost everyone needs one—to buy a new car, to purchase a home, to make a necessary home improvement, to ensure a quality education for their children, etc. That's when it's important to know what your total range of options is. And as we've seen in the preceding chapter, it's essential you understand what the costs are and how to manage those costs if you hope to avoid getting in over your head financially.

When it comes to shopping for a loan, most people are too easily intimidated. It's almost as if they see themselves asking for charity rather than as customers bringing in business and a potential profit to the bank or other creditor. They fail either to explore the available alternatives or to ask all the questions they really have about the obligations they assume, and the rights they have when taking out a loan. The net result is that often they don't get the best deal available to them.

So the first thing to keep in mind when going for a loan is that you're not going out asking someone to give you something for nothing. You're discussing a business deal that will cost you money and provide the other party a profit. It's not all that different from going out to buy a television. When you shop for a television, you look for one that suits your situation and can be depended on to work for you. And you take your budget into consideration, because what you can afford has a major effect on what you get.

Those are the same considerations to take into account when arranging a loan. You want a loan that does what you need it to do and works within your budget. And you don't want any unpleasant surprises once it's plugged in.

There are different loan options, and different places you can shop for them.

You can go to the bank and apply for a personal loan. These can range in amount from $500 to $10,000 and can be used for any worthwhile purpose. The interest rate you are charged depends on your qualifications—and, of course, the prevailing prime interest rate. Once you've filled out the loan application, you will usually know within twenty-four to forty-eight hours whether or not you've been approved. Depending again on your qualifications—that is, your general economic status—you may be required to put up some kind of collateral or to have a second party co-sign to guarantee payment in the event of your default.

Personal loans can also be arranged through a finance company. Finance companies are essentially private investors in the business of making loans to consumers looking for personal or second mortgage loans. Since they are not regulated by the banking commission, they can be more flexible when making loan decisions. But they don't give money away—they, too, want a return on their investment.

At a finance company, as at a bank, you will be rated as a credit risk. The factors considered are character, capacity, and capital: Are you responsible and trustworthy? Can you afford the loan; do you have enough income to make the payments? Do you have sufficient assets—bank accounts, car, home, stock, etc.—to put up as collateral in the event of nonpayment? Depending on their assessment of your reliability, they may require a co-signer to guarantee repayment. Those quick, "easy" loans advertised on radio and television are only quick and easy if you can satisfy the loan officer quickly and easily that you're a good credit risk. With certain less scrupulous finance companies, that can boil down to simply determining you're legally competent to sign a loan agreement and have sufficient assets to offer as collateral, which is subject to seizure in the event you can't make payments.

If you've built up a substantial credit card debt, it can make sense to take out a consolidation loan. Credit card interest rates are typically among the highest charged to consumers. If you owe $5,000 and are paying 16.8% annual interest, that's $840 interest. If you're paying 21%, as some people do, that's $1,050 in interest over the course of a year. So you can provide yourself a substantial savings by taking out a consolidation loan, paying off your credit card debt immediately in full, and then paying off the loan balance in installments at a lower rate. If the loan interest rate is 13%, that's $650 over the term of a year—$190 less than what you'd have to pay at 16.8% and $400 less than what you'd pay at 21%.

The trap to avoid falling into is running up a new series of charges on your credit cards once these are back down to a zero balance. If you do that, it won't be long before you're where you were before, but now with an additional load of debt to pay off.

A home equity loan, as we've observed, is basically a special type of personal loan for which your home serves as collateral. It's commonly advertised as a great deal for consolidating debts, with a lower interest rate than on credit accounts, plus the benefit of a tax deduction for the interest paid. This type of loan can be arranged either through a bank or finance company. Again, I recommend you avoid this type of loan as a solution to financial problems, as any further setback in an already weakened economic position exposes you immediately to the loss of your home, and just when you can least afford that.

A mortgage, of course, also entails the risk of loss of your home in the event that you cannot keep up with your payments. But a mortgage is different in that it's more commonly the loan taken out to purchase the home. Without a mortgage most people wouldn't be able to buy a house or apartment. Getting a mortgage is commonly the only way to realize the dream of home ownership, even for people with steady incomes and no financial problems. Who has the $100,000 or more needed for that just lying around?

So a mortgage is not necessarily something to avoid, because having a home of your own often depends on getting one. But here, too, you've got to shop for the best possible deal—because you don't want a mortgage you can't afford. You're working to build something up, not to dig yourself into a hole.

And then there are second mortgages. These are essentially the same as home equity loans. You offer as

collateral the equity you've built up in your home. A
first mortgage makes it possible for you to establish
that equity; a second mortgage risks what you've already established. I'm in favor of arrangements that
move you ahead; I'm not in favor of arrangements that
threaten to set you back. It's better to avoid that kind
of arrangement if you can. Look first to less risky options for obtaining the funds you need.

If you belong to a credit union, consider them as a
loan option. Credit unions generally offer low-interest
loans to members for a variety of purposes: education,
home improvement, auto, or personal.

If you're buying a new car, you may find that the
best arrangement is made through the dealer, as it's
common for manufacturers to offer low-cost car loans
as a purchase incentive, particularly in periods when
sales are slow and inventory is high.

If you have what is called a whole-life or universal
life insurance policy, you can borrow against its cash
value. The interest rates are low—generally between
5 and 8%—and the insurance company is flexible about
when you have to pay the money back, as long as the
policy stays in effect. If the loan is still outstanding
when you die, the principal and interest due will be
deducted from the benefit amount to be paid out. Your
policy's cash value builds over a period of years; what
that value is will be indicated in a table in the policy
itself. Do not confuse the cash value with the stated
benefits amount.

Some banks offer a line of credit to customers
they've determined are creditworthy. Basically that
means you can just write yourself a loan in the amount
you want up to the stated credit limit—it may be
$5,000; it may be $25,000. (Obviously, if you haven't
got an established credit history or have a poor credit

rating, this option won't be available to you.) This is an easy way to pick up a loan; it's also an easy way to work yourself into debt fast. Don't take this easy way out until you've established what it's going to cost you in interest and that you can manage repayment.

There's a similar arrangement possible for people with bank charge cards. If you have a Visa or MasterCard, you may already have received a number of special checks in the mail with your monthly statement. You use these the way you use your personal checks—to pay for a service, a purchase, or even your taxes. But instead of the check being charged to your checking account, it is charged to your credit card bill. This can be a great convenience for an "overnight loan"—a situation where you need to pay for something today and won't have the money until tomorrow. However, it's another easy way to compound your debt and eventual credit problems if your finances are shaky and repayment subsequently proves difficult.

Bank charge cards and consumer credit cards such as American Express, Diners Club, and Carte Blanche also offer you the option of obtaining a cash advance up to a stated credit limit—and depending on the outstanding balance on your card. That's great, too, if you're momentarily short of funds and need some extra cash to get you through the day, to settle an unexpected expense, or to purchase a needed item that's on special sale just when you find yourself short. It's great, that is, if your finances are in good shape and you'll be able to pay off the bill on your credit statement promptly and without difficulty. But it's a step to worse problems if you start taking cash advances when you're already having problems meeting your financial obligations. You'll only compound your debt

problems and wind up whirling full tilt on the credit
card merry-go-round before you know it, praying for
some way to get off.

What to Look for in a Loan

The Truth in Lending Act requires creditors to disclose what they charge for extending a line of credit
or a loan. These are the questions to ask when applying for a loan.

1. What is the annual percentage rate, or APR,
   you will be charged?

2. How long do you have to pay off the loan?

3. What is the total cost of the loan in dollars? (To
   figure this out, multiply the amount of your
   monthly payments by the total number
   of months payments scheduled.)

4. What is the cost of late charges for an overdue
   payment?

5. If you pay off the loan early, are there any
   prepayment penalties? (That's right, it can
   sometimes cost you extra to pay off early!)

6. Does the loan have to be secured, and if so,
   what collateral will be required?

7. Are there any other charges you have to pay?
   (With mortgages, for example, you will discover there are "points" that add to the stated
   percentage rate charged.)

Make sure you have the answers to all these questions before you take out a loan anywhere. Know every detail about what you are getting or getting into.

When it's a matter of taking a loan via an established bank or charge card credit line rather than through a separate application—and that includes taking a cash advance—take the same trouble to make sure you understand what it will cost you. You may find the price is higher than you want to pay.

Be alert to any pressures to push you into a loan arrangement that unnecessarily exposes you to higher costs.

A client asked me how to go about financing payments she faced that varied from month to month. I told her to go to her bank and apply for a credit line. With a credit line you're allowed to draw up to a stated amount—say, $10,000—but you only pay interest on the money that you use, and the rate is generally competitive.

The bank loan officer suggested that my client take out a six- to ten-year personal loan sufficient to cover her projected needs. He provided her an assurance of approval for the loan. My client came back to me, confused at the conflicting advice, and I again counseled her to go for the credit line. I pointed out that the loan officer was probably looking for the higher commission he'd earn on the personal loan and that she'd be paying interest on money borrowed that she wouldn't all need immediately.

A day or two later the woman came back to me very upset. The very same loan officer had mailed her a letter rejecting her for either loan, and she couldn't understand why, given his earlier assurances. I explained that the bank officer was angry that she hadn't opted for the loan he wanted to give her, so had decided to block any loan. Although my client didn't realize it, this is illegal.

I immediately went into action. I sent a letter of complaint to the Federal Reserve Bank, which sets standards for banking practices across the country, including documentation to show that my client had first been approved and then denied a loan. Then I contacted the bank, sending them a copy of the material forwarded to the Federal Reserve Bank. My client got her line of credit the next week. The loan officer wasn't fired, as would have been proper, so who knows how many other customers are still being subjected to pressures to take out loans that serve the bank's profit interests more than the consumer's needs.

If you are turned down after applying formally for a loan, remember you have the right to know why. If you're told it's because of a poor credit rating, remember that you're entitled to ask for a free copy of the credit report used by the creditor in making the determination to say no. (But you must ask the credit bureau for that directly. The lending institution may not legally forward a copy of your credit report to anyone else, including you.) What you find out may well be crucial to protecting your credit rating and improving your chances of acceptance on further applications. Keep in mind that some banks may turn you down simply because your report will show "too many" inquiries if you've applied to more than one institution at the same time.

9

Before You Apply for a Mortgage

Many consumers one day get to the point where they feel they're ready to shop for a home of their own. They're not experiencing immediate financial difficulties, they've got some money saved for a down payment, and they're optimistic that their regular income is sufficient and secure enough to cover prospective mortgage payments.

So off they go, heart and soul set on finding that dream house, condo, or co-op. They look around at various offerings, see a few possibilities, then start talking to real estate agents to get a fix on prices or leads in a neighborhood they find attractive. Sometimes they will spend weeks pursuing the dream before stopping to ask themselves, "Exactly how much can we afford to pay for our home?"

It's such an obvious question, and yet so many people fail to determine the answer to this question before they start on their quest.

Given some basic financial information, virtually

any real estate agent can give you a reasonable estimate on what you can afford. He or she needs to know how much money you are making, what your current obligations are, how much you owe, and how much cash you have available for the down payment and closing costs. (If you're married, your spouse's income can be figured in as well.) Using current interest rates, the agent can then figure out what you can manage in the way of mortgage payments each month. A mortgage company will generally allow you up to 25% of your gross monthly income for housing costs, and up to 36% to be allocated for total fixed debts (including your mortgage).

It's important that you complete this arithmetic *before* you start looking around, because the figure you get determines what options are realistic for you. The problem that so often arises is that consumers look around, fall in love with a house that is really beyond their means, and then decide they have to have it, no matter what. And because the real estate agent can look to a bigger commission on a more expensive house, he or she is not so inclined to rein a consumer in at this point. Determine clearly what you can afford first, and you are less likely to waste your time looking at homes that are beyond your means—or to risk committing to one that is beyond your means.

And there's another step to take before you seriously start shopping around: Get a copy of your credit report from each of the credit bureaus to make sure that everything there is current, that there's nothing that will prejudice a mortgage lender against you. A lot of consumers want a house so badly that they take the steps to that goal out of order. They invest time in house-hunting, locate the home they want, apply for a mortgage with their hopes high, and after all this get turned down because their credit record isn't clean.

Check your credit report before you take those other steps. You will save yourself more than time and heartache; you'll also save yourself the $300 (or more) fee the mortgage company will charge you just to fill out a mortgage application. If you get turned down, you lose the fee and have to start all over again.

Last year a woman came into my office very depressed and upset. She was trying to get a mortgage, after saving for many years with a good job and a high salary. She'd been turned down for a mortgage and couldn't understand why. Although she had only a single MasterCard and had never missed a payment on her account, the mortgage company told her there was something on her credit report that disqualified her from getting the mortgage she wanted. The mortgage company, of course, could not provide her with a copy of the report, as the Federal Privacy Act forbids third parties—anyone other than the credit bureau—from passing along these records.

The woman was distraught. She knew there was an error on her record but didn't know how to go about determining what it was and correcting it. That's because she didn't know she herself was entitled to ask the credit bureau for a copy of the credit report upon being rejected for the mortgage loan.

We arranged to get a copy of her report. When she brought it in to me, I took a look and burst out laughing. What did I find so amusing? she wanted to know.

I pointed out the error compromising her credit rating: A department store account opened in 1959 and closed in 1988 with an unpaid balance due was listed in her report. That was something of a joke, as in 1959 my client was only three years old. She'd never had an account at the department store.

We contacted the credit bureau to have the error rectified, and thirty days later the woman got her mortgage from the same mortgage company that had previously turned her down. When I spoke to an officer at the mortgage company, he admitted that the only thing they ever looked at on a credit report was the ratings column. They made no effort to review or understand any other part of it.

Here's a perfect example of why you should run your own credit check before you apply for a mortgage, even if you're convinced your ratings are all excellent. A stupid mistake on someone else's part could torpedo your mortgage application at the last minute.

If there's a problem with your credit rating, don't look to the real estate agent to smooth things over for you. The real estate agent is not the lender and cannot guarantee you will get the loan.

However, there are mortgage companies who will do a preliminary "qualifying" check even before you look for a house. Some mortgage companies specialize in this. Inquire around in the area where you live. Find out what the cost of such a check will be. It may be worth it to get pre-approval for a mortgage before you put in the time and emotions that always go into home-buying.

Checking credit reports can be very useful for people who don't draw a regular salary—salesmen on commission or self-employed individuals. Lenders tend to be nervous about the income security of such people; they will commonly require copies of your tax returns for the previous two years and do a special credit check with all of the credit bureaus, not just one. That can take a lot of time, so it's to your advantage here to have done the legwork on your own in advance.

If your credit report does correctly indicate a delinquent account, it's still possible to arrange a mortgage through some lenders, but the cost may well be a much higher interest rate, depending on the credit problem indicated in your file. If you know there is a problem and want to handle things in the best way, contact the creditor, negotiate a payment plan or settlement of your account, then ask the creditor to write a letter acknowledging that you are currently fulfilling your obligations. (You may have to make several monthly payments before you can elicit that letter.) At the same time, write a letter to the mortgage company explaining why you were late on any delinquent account. The mortgage company may find this acceptable in determining whether you qualify for a loan.

Save yourself trouble and disappointment. Before you invest time and energy in efforts to buy a home, determine clearly what you can afford by way of mortgage payments. Then ascertain that your credit record is clear. If it is not, take whatever steps are necessary to explain and/or resolve outstanding debts. It doesn't make sense to attempt to buy a home until you've taken care of these essential preliminaries—because they determine whether you actually can buy that home you dream of.

10

Women and Credit

The Equal Opportunity Act became federal law in 1975 and makes discrimination on the basis of sex or marital status illegal. As a result of this law, women are afforded protection in a number of important ways with respect to their treatment by creditors.

- A creditor may not ask you what your marital status is if you are applying for a separate, unsecured credit account.

- A creditor may not refuse you credit because you choose to use your maiden name instead of your married name, or use your first name with your husband's last name—for example, Mary Smith rather than Mrs. John Smith.

- A change in marital status may not be cited as justification for making you reapply for credit. In other words, if you are newly married, divorced, separated, or widowed, a creditor may not require you to make a new application before extending you further credit under a credit agreement in effect at the time your status changed.

- Creditors may not ask any question regarding your childbearing or birth practices. They may not deny you credit because you are of childbearing age and thus apt to stop working, causing your income to fall.

- A creditor must consider alimony, child support, or separate maintenance payments as legitimate income as long as the payments are regular. However, you do not have to reveal income that comes from these sources, unless you think you won't obtain credit without doing so, as your income level will otherwise appear too low.

- A creditor may not refuse to consider income that comes from a regular part-time job.

- A creditor may not require your husband to cosign or guarantee credit on a loan, unless you are depending upon his income to support your obligation, or jointly held property is to be offered as collateral for a secured loan.

If you encounter creditors who violate your rights to equal treatment in any of the above instances, immediately contact the appropriate government agency.

11

Managing Your Credit Cards

Let's assume now that your credit is clear and you are concerned about getting the best deal on credit cards, as well as understanding the eventual charges you may be subject to.

The first thing to realize is that you have a significant range of options. When it comes to applying for a bank credit card, many people assume they will do best by referring to their local bank, especially if they already have other accounts established there. They take it for granted that there's a standard rate of interest and thus very little point to shopping around.

First of all, here again you should realize that bank credit cards are an important source of income to the banks. They're not doing you a favor in issuing you a card; they're setting up an account on which they expect to make money. Extending credit is big business, and banks make millions of dollars of profit in this area. Because of the profit potential, they compete for credit accounts, and you can take advantage of that.

Banks are also subject to various regulations by state banking commissions. Among these are caps on the amount of interest a bank may charge customers on credit accounts.

Because of competition in local areas, it pays to compare costs on credit accounts from one bank to another in your community. Because there are varying limits from state to state on the interest and fees a bank may charge its credit customers, it also pays to check out possibilities across the country. Caps on interest rates now range anywhere from around 13% to 21%.

Don't worry about having an established account at a bank. Your own bank won't extend you an unsecured credit account if your credit rating is bad. If your credit rating is good, banks that you've never heard of will be glad to consider your application. Many newspapers periodically provide comparative listings of rates locally in their financial pages. Some newspapers, as well as a number of financial publications, regularly list banks around the country currently offering the best rates. Your local public library probably subscribes to one or more of these publications.

When shopping for the best credit card deal, ask yourself the following questions.

- What annual service fee will you have to pay? Fees commonly range up to $45 or more a year. Some banks will offer new accounts an exemption from the annual fee for the first year.

- What effective annual rate of interest will you be charged on outstanding balances? Interestingly, the same bank may offer different rates between different classes of the same card. Someone with a Gold MasterCard or Visa often pays as much as 3% less in interest charges than the holder of a regular MasterCard or Visa card from the same bank. Of course, credit qualifications are higher for the Gold card, so you may not have the option of choosing a Gold card account.

- When do interest charges go into effect? With many, but not all, banks, you're charged no interest if you pay off your statement fully each month within the indicated billing period.

- What transaction fees will you be subject to in addition to interest charges? For example, you will find that taking out a cash advance on your MasterCard or Visa account will incur an additional fee in almost all cases.

- What additional late fees will you incur in addition to accumulated interest charges if you don't pay at least the minimum due before the end of the billing period? Recently, more and more banks have decided to impose a $10 penalty for late payments. Some banks merely allow the interest charge to accumulate and indicate a doubled minimum payment due on the next statement. (Note, however, that most banks reserve the right to require immediate payment of the full amount due once an account is delinquent for more than one billing period.)

Now, if you're someone who has a good credit record, you may find banks—and now other institutions—from across the country offering you a credit card for general use without your solicitation. Naturally that offer is designed to prove as attractive as possible. A list of benefits will be prominently displayed: credit line, card registration services, travel insurance, shopping services, even mileage credit on an airline frequent flyer program. The cost factors may not be so clearly spelled out. Until recently it was possible for institutions to offer credit accounts through the mail without having to state the interest percentage you'd be charged on that account.

The offer of a pre-approved credit line is particularly enticing to some people. The creditor tells you that you qualify for a credit line of $2,500, $5,000, or even $10,000; you've been pre-approved; all you have to do is sign the application provided and mail it back in the postage-paid envelope included for your convenience. Having that ready credit line is such a temptation for many people that they jump at the offer. It isn't until they've gotten the card and started running up charges that they discover the costs involved. By that time they're pretty well hooked. Some people wind up with as many as five or six bank credit cards, excited at the prospect of the thousands of dollars in available credit offered, forgetting that every one of those cards represents a potential fat profit to the issuing institution—a profit that comes straight out of the consumer's pocket.

Don't get lured into a credit arrangement you can't afford. Be sure you're informed about all the charges you will be subject to before you apply for any card.

Institutions that issue credit cards are obliged to send both a complete statement of policies and obligations relating to the account and to provide monthly billing statements indicating account particulars and charges in largely standardized format. Most people throw away the "agreement" that comes with a credit card upon issuance—it's one of those small-print documents they find difficult and useless to understand. That might not be so bad if at the same time they took the trouble to understand their billing statement, which reflects the policies spelled out in detail in the consumer agreement.

Unfortunately, 80% of the people who get credit bills don't know how to read or understand them. The only figures they clearly relate to are the total balance and the minimum payment due, and they don't really understand what happens with the total balance if that's not completely paid off right away. That total balance is a figure with a life of its own—it just keeps growing. The irony of it is that the Truth in Lending Act requires credit bills to be presented in such a way that every consumer can understand them.

Let's go over the typical credit bill section by section. The positioning of items may vary somewhat from one account to another, but all will have the same indicated items.

These are the items that appear in either the upper or lower portion of your statement:

- *Name and address.* Check that they are given correctly. If you're a Robert Smith, Sr., and there's a Robert Smith, Jr., living with you and he has his own credit account, make sure you're each clearly identified.

- *Your account number.* Make sure that this corresponds to the number on your charge card.

- *Statement closing date.* This is last day for which any transactions are indicated. Any transactions posted after that date will not appear until your next statement.

- *Payment due date.* This is the day by which your payment must be *received* (not just mailed) if you are to stay current on your account. Receipt after this date subjects you to any late fee that may be charged.

- *Minimum payment.* This is the amount you must pay to stay current on your account and avoid any late fee.

- *Past due amount.* This is the amount indicated as a minimum payment on the previous billing statement but not received by the bank (or other creditor) by the payment due date indicated on that statement. Although separately indicated, it will be included in the minimum payment due in the current month.

- *Credit line/total credit.* This is the maximum debt you are allowed on this account and includes any accumulated interest and fees.

- *Available/unused credit.* This is the difference between your credit limit and what you currently owe.

- *New balance.* This is the total amount owed as of the statement closing date. Even if you pay this amount, it's possible there may be an outstanding transaction or, in some cases, that interest charges will accumulate between the statement closing date and receipt of your payment. In either case, even if there is no other activity on your account during the billing period, the next statement will still show a balance owed.

- *Previous balance.* This is the figure that appeared as "new balance" on the previous month's statement—the total you owed at that time.

- *Payments and credits.* This is the amount received from you during the preceding billing period and may also include any adjustments made in rectifying previous billing errors or disputed items. (Those adjustments, of course, depend in large part on your being alert to errors or taking the initiative in disputing any questionable item.)

- *Purchases and advances* (sometimes given in separate columns), or *debits.* The amount here represents the sum total of items charged during the billing period and cash advances you took out during that period. It does not include any finance charges or transaction fees. It may include an adjustment on a previously disputed item where the bank credited you but, upon investigation, subsequently concluded the charge to you was correct. Any annual fee will also be included here automatically during whatever month that is assessed, and possibly any late charges you may be assessed. (However, these must also be identified in the transaction record for the month.)

- *Finance charge.* This is the amount you are being charged in transaction fees (if any) and interest for the billing period covered by the statement. In addition to specifying the amount of the charge, your statement must indicate how the charge was computed. The next series of items details that.

- *Monthly periodic rate.* This is the interest charge for the month, expressed as a percentage of the total balance subject to any finance charge. If the monthly periodic rate is 1.40%, that means you are charged 1.4 cents that month on every dollar subject to a finance charge.

- *Nominal annual percentage rate.* This is what that charge amounts to in terms of an annual percentage rate—it's the monthly periodic rate multiplied by 12. It's "nominal" in that the monthly periodic rate is subject to adjustment, so that what you actually pay in terms of percentage over the course of a year may vary—be higher or lower, depending on the direction of the adjustment. If the monthly periodic rate is 1.40%, the nominal annual percentage rate is 16.8%. That means, assuming no change in the monthly rate, over the course of a year it costs you 16.8 cents in interest charges to sustain every dollar of debt. Some credit cards carry an annual interest charge as high as 21%.

- *Balance to which periodic rate was applied/Balance subject to finance charges.* This is an "average daily balance" of money outstanding on your account during the billing period, as determined by a method of calculation indicated on the reverse of your bill. It is often greater than either the previous amount due and the present "new balance." This is because a portion of the previous amount can be added to the current balance since your payment on last month's statement is rarely received until several days into the billing period covered by this month's statement.

- *Minimum transaction fee.* This is the amount or percentage you will be charged as a minimum for indicated transactions in any month that a finance charge applies. On bank credit cards you will generally see a minimum amount—50 cents is common—indicated as the minimum charge on purchase transactions for any month that a finance charge applies. (If you begin the month with a $0 balance and pay all purchase charges incurred during the period by the payment due date, often you avoid any finance charge.) For cash advances, a fee of 2% of the amount advanced or $2 (whichever is higher) is customarily charged.

- *Code/method of calculation.* This is the letter key indicating which explanation on the back of the bill details how transaction fees and the balance subject to finance charges are determined. You just about need an accounting degree to work out the figures for yourself.

In the middle of your statement you will find a large section given over to a review of all transactions recorded during the indicated billing period. This provides you the opportunity to check off the individual items charged to your account—to confirm that no items are included that do not belong to you and to confirm that the amount your account has been debited is correct in each case.

Here's where a lot of consumers get careless. They don't check to be certain that only charges for which

they are responsible are listed. They don't check that
the amounts charged are all correct.

While banks and other creditors are generally conscientious with respect to ensuring accuracy in their
billing statements, mistakes do occur. For example, an
inadvertently transposed account number somewhere
may result in someone else's purchase being billed to
you. Things like that happen regularly. And then
there's the matter of credit card fraud. A dishonest
merchant may alter the amount indicated as due on
the copy of the credit slip he submits to the credit
card company for payment. An unauthorized individual may get hold of your credit card number and
run up charges against your account. If you're not
alert to these possibilities, you could wind up a
loser.

The transaction summary commonly includes the
following details.

- *The transaction or posting date.* The transaction
  date is the day on which you actually made your
  purchase or took the indicated cash advance.
  The posting date is the date on which the transaction was recorded on your account. While past
  practice was to charge you interest from the
  posting date, not the transaction date, some
  banks have recently begun charging interest
  from the transaction date. (That's right—they
  start collecting on money they haven't even laid
  out yet!)

  Some credit statements include only the posting date, which occasionally confuses consumers
  who check the transaction record on their statements against their copy of the credit slip issued
  on the day of the transaction. They see that the

dates don't jibe, without understanding how that can be. In most cases the posting date will be a few days later than the transaction date recorded on your credit slip. Occasionally merchants or suppliers delay turning in their copy of the credit slip by as much as two weeks. On statements from banks that charge interest from the transaction date, no separate posting date is indicated.

- *Description of the transaction.* This is often no more than the name of the merchant or supplier and the city in which they are located. Usually that is enough to identify a transaction, but sometimes it gets a bit more difficult. Some companies maintain several business operations under a variety of names while handling billing from a central location that is differently identified in the transaction record. For example, this sometimes happens in the restaurant business—you go to an eatery called Sweet Sue's in one town, but the transaction record shows a charge to Comestibles, Inc., at another location. If you keep copies of your credit slips, a crosscheck will generally be enough to clear up any confusion.

  Note that this section of the transaction record not only includes mention of every use of your credit card posted in the period, but also includes a record of payment received—the date and the amount—and mention of any fees that apply besides the finance charge for that month.

- *Reference number.* The credit institution assigns every transaction (including payments) a reference number. This enables them to locate the record of the transaction easily in their computer files.

- *Debits and credits.* The amount of each transaction is given in a column directly to the right of the transaction descriptions. Check to see that the figure indicated corresponds to the figure on your copy of the credit slip.

Now, suppose that you discover there's a mistake somewhere or that charges you haven't authorized are being debited to your account. What do you do then?

Virtually every institution issuing a credit card lists an 800 number you can call to inquire about discrepancies on your statement. A call is often enough to alert the institution to review the account and take suitable action. However, it is *not* enough to protect your rights in the event that no action, or the wrong action, is taken.

The Fair Credit Billing Act gives you the right to withhold payment on a disputed item on your bill, but you preserve that right only by providing written notification within thirty days of the date on which the statement was sent out. (Again, a certified letter is always best.) In return, the card issuer must acknowledge the dispute within thirty days. At that time they can either agree with you and correct the statement in writing or not agree with you. If they don't agree, they must be able to document any claim that the charge is proper. During the dispute they may not report your account as delinquent to a credit bureau or turn it over to a collection agency. The dispute must be resolved within ninety days.

In the event of fraudulent use, you may not be held

accountable for more than $50 in charges, no matter how high the unauthorized charges to your card. But remember, the card issuer is only fully obliged to take appropriate action upon receipt of written notice, and that must be received within thirty days of when the statement was mailed out. You can't always count on a phone call to resolve a problem, and just making a phone call doesn't protect you against possible liability for the charges. It is, however, a good idea to follow up a written notice with a telephone call to be sure your letter was received and is being acted on.

Obviously the card issuer will take action to verify any claim you make regarding an error on your statement. Where those involve a transaction directly using your card, having a copy of the credit slip issued can simplify the matter. To begin with, that makes it possible for you to establish for yourself that there is an error in the charge.

Unfortunately, people are often careless with their copy of the credit slip issued when they use their card. That's your proof of purchase, indicating the date of the transaction, the merchant or supplier of the goods or services purchased, and the amount to be charged to your account. In the event that the amount charged for a transaction seems incorrect, it's by referring to your credit slip that you verify the correct charge. Don't throw away your copy of the credit slip until you've checked off the corresponding charge on your monthly statement.

When a credit slip is made up for a purchase, be sure that any carbons are either destroyed immediately or given to you. Nowadays you can order anything from soup to airline tickets simply by giving a credit card number over the telephone. Too often it happens that consumers' account numbers are obtained from carelessly discarded credit slip carbons, and before they know it, they're being billed for hundreds, even thousands of dollars in charges that come as a total surprise. Sure, if they can point to fraudulent use, they'll only be liable for up to $50 of those charges, but who needs that expense, added to the hassle of verification and then getting a new account number and card assigned?

You should also be very careful about giving credit card numbers over the telephone to unfamiliar companies or individuals who are soliciting your business. Recently a scandal erupted in connection with certain travel companies charging consumers unexplained high fees for services offered via telephone marketing. It's not always easy to dispute unexpected charges incurred in connection with a service you admit to having ordered.

Credit cards are a useful convenience for most of us. But they are a convenience with a price tag attached, and the cost of carelessness in using them can be shocking. You can find yourself paying hundreds of dollars in interest charges over the course of a year. If you fall behind on your payments, you can ruin your credit rating. If you're not attentive to the charges that appear on your statement or do not keep records of your transactions, you can wind up out-of-pocket as a result of others' mistakes or fraudulent actions. If your account number or the card itself gets into the wrong hands, there's the hassle of confirming the unauthorized use, getting a new account, and still paying the $50 cost that can be charged to you.

Shop for the best deal on credit cards. Use them wisely. Keep track of every charge to your account.

Don't let the convenience a credit card affords blind you to the potential for financial trouble that exists if you don't manage it wisely or keep proper track of your account.

Appendix 1

Credit Bureau Addresses

The following addresses are for the national headquarters of the indicated credit bureaus. Each bureau has other regional offices scattered around the United States, and if you have the address for an office near you, you can also write to that office in connection with any inquiry or complaint. Once you begin a correspondence with a particular office, address any related correspondence there, too, unless otherwise directed, or if you are forwarding a complaint about a regional office to the national headquarters. (Remember to keep copies of all correspondence.)

Chilton Automatic
Systems
12606 Greenville Avenue
Dallas, TX 75243

Credit Bureau Inc. (CBI)
P.O. Box 4091
Atlanta, GA 30302

Leascore Inc.
3900 Ford Road, #17I
Philadelphia, PA 19131

Pinger System
2505 Fanning Street
Houston, TX 77002

Trans Union Information
444 North Michigan
Avenue
Chicago, IL 60611

TRW Credit Information
505 City Parkway West
Orange, CA 92667

The following are regional offices for the credit
bureaus listed above.

Credit Bureau Associates
(CBA)
6981 North Park Drive
East
Pennsauken, NJ 08109

TRW
5 Century Drive
Parsippany, NJ 07054

Trans Union Credit
Bureau
1211 Chestnut Street
Philadelphia, PA 19107

Appendix 2

The Fair Credit Reporting Act

Following are the major provisions of the Fair Credit Reporting Act relating to consumer credit reports. Some sections or subsections with a more specialized focus are not included here.

The Fair Credit Reporting Act comprises Title VI of the Consumer Protection Act, sections 601 through 622.

Section 602. Findings and purpose

(b) It is the purpose of this title to require that consumer reporting agencies adopt reasonable procedures for meeting the needs of commerce for consumer credit, personnel, insurance, and other information in a manner which is fair and equitable to the consumer, with regard to the confidentiality, accuracy, relevancy, and proper utilization of such information in accordance with the requirements of this title.

Section 603. Definitions and rules of construction

(b) The term "person" means any individual, partnership, corporation, trust, estate, cooperative, association, government or governmental subdivision or agency, or other entity.

(c) The term "consumer" means an individual.

(d) The term "consumer report" means any written, oral, or other communication of any information by a consumer reporting agency bearing on a consumer's credit worthiness, credit standing, credit capacity, character, general reputation, personal characteristics, or mode of living which is used or expected to be used or collected in whole or in part for the purpose of serving as a factor in establishing the consumer's eligibility for (1) credit or insurance to be used primarily for personal, family, or household purposes, or (2) employment purposes, or (3) other purposes authorized under section 604. . . .

(f) The term "consumer reporting agency" means any person which for monetary fees, dues, or on a cooperative nonprofit basis, regularly engages in whole or in part in the practice of assembling or evaluating consumer credit information or other information on consumers for the purpose of furnishing consumer reports to third parties, and which uses any means or facility of interstate commerce for the purpose of preparing or furnishing consumer reports.

(g) The term "file," when used in connection with information on any consumer, means all of the information on that consumer recorded and retained by a consumer reporting agency regardless of how the information is stored.

Section 604. Permissible purposes of reports

A consumer reporting agency may furnish a consumer report under the following circumstances and no other:

(1) In response to the order of a court having jurisdiction to issue such an order.

(2) In accordance with the written instructions of the consumer to whom it relates.

(3) To a person which it has reason to believe—

    (A) Intends to use the information in connection with a credit transaction involving the consumer on whom the information is to be furnished and involving the extension of credit to, or review or collection of an account of the consumer; or

    (B) Intends to use the information for employment purposes; or

    (C) Intends to use the information in connection with the underwriting of insurance involving the consumer; or

    (D) Intends to use the information in connection with a determination of the consumer's eligibility for a license or other benefit granted by a governmental instrumentality required by law to consider an applicant's financial responsibility or status; or

    (E) Otherwise has a legitimate business need for the information in connection with a business transaction involving the consumer.

Section 605. Obsolete information

(a) Except as authorized under subsection (b), no consumer reporting agency may make any consumer report containing any of the following items of information:

(1) Cases under Title 11 of the United States Code or under the Bankruptcy Act that, from the date of the entry of the order for relief or the date of adjudication, as the case may be, antedate the report by more than ten years.

(2) Suits and judgments which, from date of entry, antedate the report by more than seven years or until the governing statute of limitations has expired, whichever is the longer period.

(3) Paid tax liens which, from date of payment, antedate the report by more than seven years.

(4) Accounts placed for collection or charged to profit and loss which antedate the report by more than seven years.

(5) Records of arrest, indictment, or conviction of crime which, from date of disposition, release, or parole, antedate the report by more than seven years.

(6) Any other adverse item of information which antedates the report by more than seven years.

(b) The provisions of subsection (a) are not applicable in the case of any consumer credit report to be used in connection with—

(1) A credit transaction involving, or which may reasonably be expected to involve, a principal amount of $50,000 or more;

(2) The underwriting of life insurance involving, or which may reasonably be expected to involve, a face amount of $50,000 or more; or

(3) The employment of any individual at an annual

salary which equals, or which may reasonably be expected to equal $20,000, or more.

Section 607. Compliance procedures

(a) Every consumer reporting agency shall maintain reasonable procedures designed to avoid violations of section 605 and to limit the furnishing of consumer reports to the purposes listed under section 604. These procedures shall require that prospective users of the information identify themselves, certify the purposes for which the information is sought, and certify that the information shall be used for no other purpose. Every consumer reporting agency shall make a reasonable effort to verify the identity of a new prospective user and the uses certified by such prospective user prior to furnishing such user a consumer report. No consumer reporting agency may furnish a consumer report to any person if it has reasonable grounds for believing that the consumer report will not be used for a purpose listed in section 604.

(b) Whenever a consumer reporting agency prepares a consumer report it shall follow reasonable procedures to assure maximum possible accuracy of the information concerning the individual about whom the report relates.

Section 609. Disclosures to consumers

(a) Every consumer reporting agency shall, upon request and proper identification of any consumer, clearly and accurately disclose to the consumer:

   (1) The nature and substance of all information (except medical information) in its files on the consumer at the time of the request.

   (2) The sources of the information [for regular consumer reports]. . . .

(3) The recipients of any consumer report on the consumer which it has furnished—
  (A) for employment purposes within the two-year period preceding the request, and
  (B) for any other purpose within the six-month period preceding the request.

Section 610. Conditions of disclosure to consumers

(a) A consumer reporting agency shall make the disclosures required under section 609 during normal business hours and on reasonable notice.

(b) The disclosures required under section 609 shall be made to the consumer—
  (1) In person if he appears in person and furnished proper identification; or
  (2) By telephone if he has made a written request, with proper identification, for telephone disclosure and the toll charge, if any, for the telephone call is prepaid by or charged directly to the consumer.

(c) Any consumer reporting agency shall provide trained personnel to explain to the consumer any information furnished to him pursuant to section 609.

(d) The consumer shall be permitted to be accompanied by one other person of his choosing, who shall furnish reasonable identification. A consumer reporting agency may require the consumer to furnish a written statement granting permission to the consumer reporting agency to discuss the consumer's file in such person's presence.

(e) Except as provided in sections 616 and 617, no consumer may bring any action or proceeding in the nature of defamation, invasion of privacy, or negligence with respect to the reporting of information against any consumer reporting agency, any user of information, or any person who furnished information to a consumer reporting agency, based on information disclosed pursuant to section 609, 610, or 615, except as to false information furnished with malice or willful intent to injure such consumer.

Section 611. Procedure in case of disputed accuracy

(a) If the completeness or accuracy of any item of information contained in his file is disputed by a consumer, and such dispute is directly conveyed to the consumer reporting agency by the consumer, the consumer reporting agency shall within a reasonable period of time reinvestigate and record the current status of that information unless it has reasonable grounds to believe that the dispute by the consumer is frivolous or irrelevant. If after such reinvestigation such information is found to be inaccurate or can no longer be verified, the consumer reporting agency shall promptly delete such information. The presence of contradictory information in the consumer's file does not in and of itself constitute reasonable grounds for believing the dispute is frivolous or irrelevant.

(b) If the reinvestigation does not resolve the dispute, the consumer may file a brief statement setting forth the nature of the dispute. The consumer reporting agency may limit such statements to not more than one hundred words if it provides the consumer with assistance in writing a clear summary of the dispute.

(c) Whenever a statement of dispute is filed, unless there is reasonable grounds to believe that it is frivolous or irrelevant, the consumer reporting agency shall, in any subsequent consumer report containing the information in question, clearly note that it is disputed by the consumer and provide either the consumer's statement or a clear and accurate codification or summary thereof.

(d) Following any deletion of information which is found to be inaccurate or whose accuracy can no longer be verified or any notation as to disputed information, the consumer reporting agency shall, at the request of the consumer, furnish notification that the item has been deleted or the statement, codification or summary pursuant to subsection (b) or (c) to any person specifically designated to the consumer who has within two years prior thereto received a consumer report for employment purposes, or within six months prior thereto received a consumer report for any other purpose, which contained the deleted or disputed information. The consumer reporting agency shall clearly and conspicuously disclose to the consumer his rights to make such a request. Such disclosure shall be made at or prior to the time the information is deleted or the consumer's statement regarding the disputed information is received.

Section 612. Charges for certain disclosures

A consumer reporting agency shall make all disclosures pursuant to section 609 and furnish all consumer reports pursuant to section 611(d) without charge to the consumer if, within thirty days after receipt by such consumer of a notification pursuant to section 615 or notification from a debt collection agency affiliated with such consumer reporting agency stating that the consumer's credit rating may be or has been adversely affected, the consumer makes a request under section 609 or 611(d). Otherwise, the consumer reporting agency may impose a reasonable charge on the consumer for making disclosure to such consumer pursuant to section 609, the charge for which shall be indicated to the consumer prior to making disclosure; and for furnishing notifications, statements, summaries, or codifications to persons designated by the consumer pursuant to section 611(d), the charge for which shall be indicated to the consumer prior to furnishing such information and shall not exceed the charge that the consumer reporting agency would impose on each designated recipient for a consumer report, except that no charge may be made for notifying such persons of the deletion of information which is found to be inaccurate or which can no longer be verified.

Section 615. Requirements on users of consumer reports

(a) Whenever credit or insurance for personal, family, or household purposes, or employment involving a consumer is denied or the charge for such credit or insurance is increased either wholly or partly because of information contained in a consumer report from a consumer reporting agency, the user of the consumer report shall so advise the consumer against whom such adverse action has been taken and supply the name and address of the consumer reporting agency making the report.

(b) Whenever credit for personal, family, or household purposes involving a consumer is denied or the charge for such credit is increased either wholly or partly because of information obtained from a person other than a consumer reporting agency bearing upon consumer's credit worthiness, credit standing, credit capacity, character, general reputation, or mode of living, the user of such information shall, within a reasonable period of time, upon the consumer's written request for the reasons for such adverse action received within sixty days after learning of such adverse action, disclose the nature of the information to the consumer. The user of such information shall clearly and accurately disclose to the consumer his right to make such written request at the time such adverse action is communicated to the consumer.

(c) No person shall be held liable for any violation of this section if he shows by a preponderance of the evidence that at the time of the alleged violation he maintained reasonable procedures to assure compliance with the provisions of subsections (a) and (b).

Section 616. Civil liability for willful noncompliance

Any consumer reporting agency or user of information which willfully fails to comply with any requirement imposed under this title with respect to any consumer is liable to that consumer in an amount equal to the sum of—

   (1) Any actual damages sustained by the consumer as a result of the failure;

   (2) Such amount of punitive damages as the court may allow; and

   (3) In the case of any successful action to enforce any liability under this section, the costs of the action together with reasonable attorney's fees as determined by the court.

Section 617. Civil liability for negligent noncompliance

Any consumer reporting agency or user of information which is negligent in failing to comply with any requirement imposed under this title with respect to any

consumer is liable to that consumer in an amount
equal to the sum of—

(1) Any actual damages sustained by the consumer
as a result of the failure;

(2) In the case of any successful action to enforce
any liability under this section, the costs of the
action together with reasonable attorney's fees
as determined by the court.

Section 618. Jurisdiction of courts; limitation of actions

An action to enforce any liability created under this
title may be brought in any appropriate United States
district court without regard to the amount in contro-
versy, or in any other court of competent jurisdiction,
within two years from the date on which the liability
arises, except that where a defendant has materially
and willfully misrepresented any information required under this title to be disclosed to an individual
and the information so misrepresented is material to
the establishment of the defendant's liability to that
individual under this title, the action may be brought
at any time within two years after discovery by the
individual of the misrepresentation.

Section 619. Obtaining information under false pretenses

Any person who knowingly and willfully obtains information on a consumer from a consumer reporting
agency under false pretenses shall be fined not more
than $5,000 or imprisoned not more than one year, or
both.

Section 620. Unauthorized disclosures by officers or employees

Any officer or employee of a consumer reporting agency who knowingly and willfully provides information concerning an individual from the agency's files to a person not authorized to receive that information shall be fined not more than $5,000 or imprisoned not more than one year, or both.

Section 621. Administrative enforcement

(a) Compliance with the requirements imposed under this title shall be enforced under the Federal Trade Commission Act by the Federal Trade Commission with respect to consumer reporting agencies and all other persons subject thereto, except to the extent that enforcement of the requirements imposed under this title is specifically committed to some other government agency under subsection (b) hereof. . . . Any person violating any of the provisions of this title shall be subject to the penalties and entitled to the privileges and immunities provided in the Federal Trade Commission Act as though the applicable terms and provisions thereof were part of this title.

(b) Compliance with the requirements imposed under this title with respect to consumer reporting agencies and persons who use consumer reports from such agencies shall be enforced under—

   (1) Section 8 of the Federal Deposit Insurance Act, in the case of:

      (A) National banks, by the Comptroller of the Currency;

      (B) Member banks of the Federal Reserve System (other than national banks), by the Federal Reserve Board; and

   (C) Banks insured by the Federal Deposit Insurance Corporation (other than members of the Federal Reserve System), by the Board of Directors of the Federal Deposit Insurance System.

 (2) Section 5(d) of the Home Owners Loan Act of 1933, section 407 of the National Housing Act, and sections 6(i) and 17 of the Federal Home Loan Bank Act, by the Federal Home Loan Bank Board (acting directly or through the Federal Savings and Loan Insurance Corporation), in the case of any institution subject to any of those provisions;

 (3) The Federal Credit Union Act, by the Administrator of the National Credit Union Administration with respect to any Federal credit union;

 (4) The Acts to regulate commerce, by the Interstate Commerce Commission with respect to any common carrier subject to those Acts;

 (5) The Federal Aviation Act of 1958 by the Civil Aeronautics Board with respect to any air carrier or foreign air carrier subject to that Act; and

 (6) The Packers and Stockyards Act, 1921 (except as provided in section 406 of that Act), by the Secretary of Agriculture with respect to any activities subject to that Act.

Section 622. Relation to state laws

This title does not annul, alter, affect, or exempt any person subject to the provisions of this title complying with the laws of any State with respect to the collection, distribution, or use of any information on consumers, except to the extent that those laws are inconsistent with any provision of this title, and then only to the extent of the inconsistency.

Appendix 3

Sample Letters

The following are form letters you can adapt easily for your use in the indicated situation.

To request a copy of your credit report following rejection of an application for credit

Your name
Street address
City, state, ZIP

Social Security #:
Date of birth:

Name of credit bureau
Street address
City, state, ZIP

Attention: Consumer Relations Department

On (date) I received notification from (creditor name and address) that my application for a (credit account or loan) was being rejected following a review of my credit history as held on file by you.

So that I may verify the accuracy of my credit record, please forward me a copy of my credit report, in accord with the relevant provisions of the Fair Credit Reporting Act. As this request is being forwarded within 30 days of the credit rejection noted above, I understand that there is no charge to me for receipt of the report and that it will be forwarded to me within a reasonable period of time.

Thank you for your prompt cooperation.

Sincerely yours,

(Signature)

Date:

To dispute items in your credit report that are reported inaccurately

Your name
Street address
City, state, ZIP

Social Security #:
Date of birth:

Name of credit bureau
Street address
City, state, ZIP

Attention: Customer Relations Department

I recently received a copy of the report containing my credit history, and I am requesting that the following items listed in my credit report be investigated immediately. They are inaccurate as given, and the inaccuracies are most injurious to my credit record.

Subscriber name:
Subscriber code:
Account number:
Description of inaccuracy: _____
_____
_____

Subscriber name:
Subscriber code:
Account number:
Description of inaccuracy: _____
_____
_____

I understand that in accordance with federal law the

information here disputed will be checked at the
source and that I will be notified of the results of your
investigation within a reasonable length of time (30
days).

Furthermore, in accordance with the Fair Credit Reporting Act, Public Law 91-508, Title VI, Section 611,
Subsections A–D, I would like the name and business
address of each individual with whom you verified the
above item so that I can follow up appropriately.

Please forward a copy of my updated credit report after you have completed your investigation.

Your cooperation in this matter is greatly appreciated.

                              Sincerely yours,

                              (Signature)

Date:

To request removal of unauthorized credit inquiries from your credit record

Your name
Street address
City, state, ZIP

Social Security #:
Date of birth:

Name of credit bureau
Street address
City, state, ZIP

Attention: Customer Relations Department

The following credit inquiries listed on my credit report were not authorized by me, and I would like them removed from my credit record:

Subscriber name:
Subscriber code:
Date of inquiry:

Subscriber name:
Subscriber code:
Date of inquiry:

Please forward a copy of my updated credit report after you have completed your investigation.

Your cooperation in this matter is greatly appreciated.

Sincerely yours,

(Signature)

Date:

To follow up on a request for a correction in your credit report when you've received no reply after 30 days or more

Your name
Street address
City, state, ZIP

Name of credit bureau
Street address
City, state, ZIP

Attention: Consumer Relations Department

On (date) I sent a certified letter requesting that you investigate the specified inaccuracies in my credit history. To date, I have not heard from you.

Under the Fair Credit Reporting Act, I am entitled to an investigation of these items within a reasonable length of time. I believe I have waited more than a reasonable length of time and would like you to forward a report of your investigation and a copy of my corrected report immediately.

I am enclosing a copy of my earlier letter for your reference.

Your prompt attention will be most appreciated.

Sincerely yours,

(Signature)

Date:

To have a credit bureau remove any reference to a past-due account on which the last activity was more than 7 years ago

> Your name
> Street address
> City, state, ZIP
>
> Social Security #:
> Date of birth:

Name of credit bureau
Street address
City, state, ZIP

Attention: Consumer Relations Department

The account indicated below, which is referenced negatively in my credit report, has seen no activity since more than 7 years ago. Under the terms of the Fair Credit Reporting Act (Sections 605–7), a statute of limitations applies and reference to this account must be deleted from my credit report.

> Subscriber:
> Subscriber code:
> Account number:

Please delete all references to this account immediately and forward to me a copy of the corrected credit report.

Your prompt response will be greatly appreciated.

> Sincerely yours,
>
> (Signature)

Date:

**To have a creditor instruct a credit bureau to re-
move any reference to a past-due account on which
the last activity was more than 7 years ago**

Credit Manager
Name of creditor
Street address
City, state, ZIP

Re: Statute of limitations in application to the follow-
     ing account
     Your name as given on the account record
     Account #:

Dear Sir/Madam:

   In reviewing the credit file held on me by (name of
credit bureau), I have discovered a continuing reference to the account noted above, even though the last
activity on that account was more than 7 years ago.
   Under the Fair Credit Reporting Act, no account may
properly be maintained on a credit report beyond 7
years after the date of last activity. The continued inclusion of the above account on my credit report is in
clear violation of the express terms of the law. Moreover, that inclusion is injurious to my credit profile
and is hindering me in efforts to establish new lines
of credit.
   I have been advised by (name of credit bureau) that
they must be contacted by you to have this account
removed from my credit report.
   I would appreciate your cooperation in having this
negative account removed from my credit report immediately, in accordance with the applicable terms of
the Fair Credit Reporting Act.

                                        Sincerely yours,

                                        (Signature)

Date:

To notify a creditor that you cannot keep up with current obligations and to ask for an extension of time in which to meet those

Date

Credit Manager
Name of creditor
Street address
City, state, ZIP

Re: Account # (give number) in the name of (give your
     name as it appears on your account records)

Dear Sir/Madam:

I have overextended my credit to the point where it is not possible for me to meet my current obligations.

I am asking for an extension of time to meet my obligations. I owe you approximately (give amount).

I have carefully analyzed my income, living expenses, and debts, and have determined that I will be able to forward a monthly payment of (indicate amount). I will mail you this amount as a minimum every month—and more when possible—until my indebtedness is paid off.

If you have any further questions, I would be pleased to discuss my account with you at any time. I appreciate your patience and courtesy and hope I may look forward to your cooperation.

Sincerely yours,

(Signature)

**To notify a creditor of your good faith in wishing
to pay off a past-due debt in installments**

                                          Date

Credit Manager
Name of creditor
Street address
City, state, ZIP

Re: Payments on past-due account # (give number) in
    the name of (give name as it appears on the ac-
    count records)

Dear Sir/Madam:

In order to remain in good standing with your company, despite unforeseen circumstances that have
arisen in the past, I wish to make a series of regular
payments until the outstanding balance on my account is paid in full.

I will make payments every (specify time period) in
the amount of (specify amount). I will not miss a payment. I hope that this good-faith effort will lead you
to reconsider upgrading my credit rating with the
credit bureau to which you subscribe.

Your understanding and cooperation in this matter
are greatly appreciated.

                                          Sincerely yours,

                                          (Signature)

To offer a lump-sum settlement of a past-due account in exchange for the creditor's restoring your credit rating

Date

Credit Manager
Name of creditor
Street address
City, state, ZIP

Re: Settlement of past-due account # (give number) in name of (give name as it appears on account records)

Dear Sir/Madam:

I am willing and able to make a lump-sum payment for a full and final settlement of the entire indebtedness in the amount of (indicate total). I am prepared to make full settlement upon your assurance that your company will restore a favorable credit rating in connection with this account.

If a settlement on this basis is acceptable to your company, please have an authorized representative of your company indicate agreement by signing this letter and returning the original to me. (Please hold a copy for your files.) Upon receipt of the countersigned letter, I will forward a check in payment of the full amount due by return mail.

If you have any questions or would like to discuss this matter further, please do not hesitate to contact me.

Sincerely yours,

(Signature)

The undersigned authorized representative hereby
agrees to a settlement of this account on the terms
stated above, including, in particular, restoration of a
favorable credit rating for the account holder upon
receipt of the indicated amount due.

_____

Authorized signature

_____

Date

To register a complaint with the Federal Trade Commission regarding harassment by a debt collection agency

Date

Your name
Street address
City, state, ZIP

Federal Trade Commission
Pennsylvania Avenue and 6th Street, N.W.
Washington, D.C. 20580

Re: Complaint of harassment in violation of the Fair
      Debt Collection Practices Act

Dear Sir/Madam:

I believe that the Fair Debt Collection Practices Act is
being violated by (give name of collection agency) located at (give address).

(Collection agency name) has harassed me with the
following debt collection practices: (List each action,
the person involved, and the date and time of the action.)

I have requested (name of collection agency) to stop
their actions and informed them of the laws protecting consumers against such harassment, but they are
continuing their actions. I believe they may be using
the same harassing tactics in dealing with other consumers.

I ask that you investigate the business practices of

(name of collection agency) and impose appropriate sanctions to eliminate their unfair debt-collection activities.

Sincerely yours,

(Signature)

cc: (Collection agency)
    (The original creditor on the account)